AGAINST THE TIDE, TOWARDS THE KINGDOM

NML NEW MONASTIC LIBRARY
Resources for Radical Discipleship

For over a millennium, if Christians wanted to read theology, practice Christian spirituality, or study the Bible, they went to the monastery to do so. There, people who inhabited the tradition and prayed the prayers of the church also copied manuscripts and offered fresh reflections about living the gospel in a new era. Two thousand years after the birth of the church, a new monastic movement is stirring in North America. In keeping with ancient tradition, new monastics study the classics of Christian reflection and are beginning to offer some reflections for a new era. The New Monastic Library includes reflections from new monastics as well as classic monastic resources unavailable elsewhere.

Against the Tide, Towards the

KINGDOM

JENNY &
JUSTIN DUCKWORTH

Foreword by
CHARLES RINGMA

CASCADE *Books* · Eugene, Oregon

AGAINST THE TIDE, TOWARDS THE KINGDOM

New Monastic Library 8

Cascade Books
An Imprint of Wipf and Stock Publishers
199 W. 8th Ave., Suite 3
Eugene, OR 97401

www.wipfandstock.com

ISBN 13: 978-1-60899-867-8

Cataloging-in-Publication data:

Duckworth, Jenny.

Against the tide, towards the kingdom / Jenny and Justin Duckworth; foreword by Charles Ringma.

xviii + 112 p. ; 23 cm.

New Monastic Library 8

ISBN 13: 978-1-60899-867-8

1. Urban Vision. 2. Monastic and religious life—New Zealand. I. Duckworth, Justin. II. Ringma, Charles. III. Title. IV. Series.

BV4406.N45 D80 2011

Manufactured in the U.S.A.

We dedicate this book to Johnny Te Awhe. Our prayer is to strengthen all who are rowing their waka, *that they might continue to pull those who are drowning out of the water.*

CONTENTS

This book will sit lightly, easily, and happily in your hands. And its lilting storytelling will bring a smile to your face and joy to your heart. This is because this book is such a good read. And its pages are full of wisdom, goodness and hope.

I began my introduction of this book on this note because this is what helps make the book rather unusual. People who are into radical Christian discipleship are not always characterized by joy and down-to-earth simplicity and practicality. Often such Christians are rather "heavy duty" in their approach to life. They are intense rather than wise, ministry-focused rather than life-oriented, somber rather than joyful. They are seeking to make the world right and good and just, and this is often seen as a very serious and burdensome task

This story of Justin and Jenny Duckworth and the development of Urban Vision just does not have such a flavor. The tone is very different. Here are a group of Christians who are seeking to live the gospel in the modern world in the joy of the kingdom of God. Here are the stories of a group of New Zealand radicals, primarily in the Wellington area, living a costly incarnational vision of serving the poor. But they do so in the solidarity of friendship and in the easier rhythm of not taking themselves too seriously. They learn from their mistakes and they don't think they have all the answers for society. They just want to follow Jesus and serve the neighbor, particularly the neglected neighbor in our urban world.

But make no mistake there is nothing lightweight or simplistic about this book. This is a testament of a very long journey in the following of Christ, in the forging of Christian communities, and in the challenge of serving the poor. Thus these pages are laden with a wisdom forged out of obedience, service, and suffering. And that is like finding gold.

The story of this couple and of this home-grown missional movement with the marks of a new Protestant religious order, touches on the whole gamut of life, service, and spirituality. As such this book can be put into the hands of any searching young person with the question: "Do you want to know how to live for Christ in the twenty-first century?" Here, read this book.

This book therefore is full of insight in how urban mission can be done well. It is brimming with wisdom about relationships. It is full of insights regarding the joys and challenges of building Christian community. And there is practical advice on leadership, the practice of hospitality, various spiritual disciplines, and the setting of boundaries.

And there is more. Networking. Conflict resolution. Celebration. Creativity. Counselling. Retreats. Family. Work. Sexuality. Money. Sacrifice. Prayer. Sabbath. No wonder this is such a rich story. This is not just a story of service. It is a story of living a life, of following Christ, and of being workers in the cause of peace and justice. This story of being, living, and serving weaves a communal identity and spirituality. As such, it overcomes our narrow individualism

The delightful idiosyncratic Urban Vision story is nevertheless part of a worldwide movement where contemporary Christians are seeking to live a greater fidelity to the gospel and are seeking to live against the tide of a soulless Western capitalism and a dysfunctional consumerism.

Some of the hallmarks of this broader movement are reflected in this book. A recovery of the centrality of Christ. A call to live the gospel, not just believe the gospel. The challenge to do things together, to live in community and to be in solidarity, rather than to live our fractured individualism. The invitation to serve the poor as a way of serving Christ himself. The challenge to journey with the neighbor, rather than just to provide programs of help. The call to discover a deeper spirituality that will bring glory to God, will make us more attentive to the Spirit, and will be bread and wine for the journey. The invitation to live a more sacramental way of life. The challenge in the work of evangelization and justice to transform broken lives and communities into persons and places of healing and hope. And the call to a simple lifestyle and a care for the earth that joins us with God's concern for all that was made and for all that needs careful sustenance and renewal.

May this book then sit lightly in your hands. May it challenge your heart. May it reorient your footsteps. May it invite you to live in a similar way.

—Charles Ringma, urban and cross-cultural missioner and theologian.

ACKNOWLEDGMENTS

The big love goes to all those who have travelled in Urban Vision on this *waka* with us. If I had been writing simply a memoir I would have of course included all your names and faces and colourful dramas that we have shared over the many years; they remain in my filled-up photo books and my bulging memories. And we all know that we would never have started or at least never continued without those who have cheered us on, picked us up, and called us on again. So here's to you Charles, Rita, Mick, Ruby, Lois, Dave, John, Karen, Henry, Joseph, Catherine, Jenny, Bishop Tom, Uncle Mowhi, Michael and Daryl. Thanks Charles for your confidence that our story was worth writing down and to Karen my new friend and editor for working with the rough musings of us "give it a go" kiwis. Thanks Amber for attending to all the details of our life, including this book. And to our young people, our neighbours and friends who have come to find shelter and hospitality, you have changed our lives forever now; you have ruined us for normal life because you have been gifts from God. God is generous, God is good.

Recently, Justin and I packed up our kids and our backpacks for a sabbatical year, heading far away from our home at the bottom (or top) of the world to find our souls again, to be inspired by God and his people in other places. As we got chatting with folks around the world, we found ourselves telling the story of our life with Urban Vision in New Zealand/ Aotearoa, which began as an experiment in a poorer suburb of Wellington city over fifteen years ago with a group of friends who wanted a bit more than Sunday church.

So many of the young adults in church (then and now) were waiting for their lives to happen. "One day I hope to . . ." "When I grow up . . ." or "When I'm really ready . . ." There is a long list of sensible things to do first. "I need to start my study, I need to finish my study, I need to pay off my student loan, I need to save for my Overseas Experience (hereafter, OE), I need to do my OE, I need to start my career, I need to plan for my wedding, I need time within my new marriage, I need to start my family, I need to get my kids through the preschool years, I need be there for my kids as they approach their high school years, I need to look after my aging parents, I need to save for my kids' university, I need a few years to recover from all those busy years, I need to restart my career and my marriage and get through my mid-life transition still feeling like I have something to offer, I need to work hard to maintain my standard of living, I need to support my grown up kids and grandchildren, I need to die. . ."

But we decided early on we couldn't wait. We were young, but we were getting older fast. We didn't want to wake up one day to realize we had drifted through life in a cultural shape we didn't even believe in. We didn't want to waste our high-energy years waiting to be mature enough.

In fact Justin remembers the scary day, while in deep discussion with friends over the poverty and injustice of the world, when he realized that someone was going to have to start living the alternative—and that someone had to be us. We wondered if we could live our lives with a fully focused kingdom agenda and then add the other list of things around the edge, rather than the other way around. Maybe our parents could be blessed by our commitment to live out this kingdom culture. Maybe our children could grow up within it and our marriage flourish along the way. Maybe our careers could serve our calling.

We had been raised in Youth for Christ, so approaching our lives with a sense of calling came naturally. Whether or not there were grants, financial support or money miracles (and we did experience all three at some time), we did it anyway. With other youth workers, we developed a community around our shared households, all within walking distance, and began a rhythm of prayer and communication.

Finances were always tight, so when we moved into an amazing home for teenage girls as part of our youth work, we shared rooms with the young women to save on rent. Some people found this outrageous, but we found it helpful to getting alongside them and sharing all of our lives together, nailing our own sense of "my rights" to the cross. We also became good at taking long walks and finding places to hide. Over time, we moved into the inner city, living with far too many folks in a old mattress factory, then taking over the houses next door. Sharing meals and life with street people, sex workers, council tenants, and many other wandering types, we had become more than youth workers, so we left our YFC Wellington connection with deep gratitude and became "Urban Vision," our own charitable trust.

Over the years, our community have focused on a beautiful *whakatauki*—old Māori wisdom from here in New Zealand—that frames our community's values: *Kotahi te kohao o te ngira e kuhuna ai te miro ma, te miro pango te miro whero,* which translates: "There are three strands but they form one thread which goes through the eye of the needle." This speaks to us of our personal relationship with Jesus, our relationship with other believers, and our relationship with others who are suffering in this hurting world. And the eye of the needle remains a biblical challenge for us Western Christians and our wealthy load!

As we follow the life of Jesus, we notice him nurturing, protecting, attending to his own relationship with God. We see him stealing away to be alone, to pray, to listen, to wrestle, to discern—even when he is busy! We see him share life with a few and make them his best friends—not a particularly talented or specialized bunch, but his bunch. They take the journey together, up and down, good and bad, making the ordinary extraordinary. Together, they go to the edge, tending to those who are broken and hurting, rejected and sick. These three strands guide our community along the path of what it means to follow Jesus. You don't have to be skilled or know much about this stuff, but we ask people to give all three a go together. That's who we are and that's what we believe in. The question is not, should I live like this or not, but, if not here then where? If not this way, then how else can we work these three components into our lives? If not with these friends, then with whom? None of it is optional but there are many, many ways it could look, each a unique invitation from God himself.

Around the world, there is a new movement of the Spirit, called by some new monasticism, by others the missional or emerging church, and by still others radical community. This is a movement we feel at home within, for it takes the good things of the old ways and reshapes them for new and challenging times. As we traveled, we met so many people who were interested in this new way of doing, or being, church, and we enjoyed finding ourselves in the middle of these conversations with people who were asking the same questions we had asked. So what does it mean to live as Jesus lived? To relocate to the margins? To hang out with the socially outcast? To challenge the powers of the day? To be hated and rejected for the sake of the gospel? To preach both grace and truth? Did Jesus call us to be normal, to fit right into the middle of our culture as good upright citizens? To do life the way the politicians, the media, and the consumer leaders would invite us to? Does following Jesus mean being a good friend, a good spouse, a good parent, a good child, a good church attendee, a good employee, a good citizen? Does it mean doing this system we have well? Or does following Jesus take us outside this system around us to a different way of life? What does it mean to make disciples? To preach good news to the poor? To bind up the broken hearted? To produce the fruit of the spirit? To mature our character through sacrifice? To pick up our cross daily? To trust him to meet our needs? To know his resurrection power, to do miracles greater than these?

As we re-told the story of our past fifteen years with Urban Vision, we came to realize that we had learnt quite a bit—often through our mistakes and failures—and we also discovered that people were interested in hearing about and learning from stories like ours. The world is full of desperate needs, and kingdom answers come in all shapes and sizes, so I share our story not to bring glory to ourselves but to remember and bear witness to God's faithfulness to us, in the hope of inspiring more "want to be radical followers of Jesus" to give it a go.

We are not super stars. We are just ordinary Wellingtonians from different walks of life, trying to live together in a way that embraces those in our neighborhoods who are struggling, living out the good news we have found. It amazes us that God has been able to pull us together to create this small community of prayer, creativity, and action we call Urban Vision. Nowadays we are in six neighborhoods and have a piece of land, Ngatiawa (People of the River), an old Presbyterian camp that's become a contemplative space for friends and neighbors from the city teams, a haven for people needing a place to reflect and recreate, a contemporary monastery, if you like, with a rhythm of daily prayer. But our only boast is that we heard an invitation from God and gave it a go. And when it all went badly, we picked ourselves up and gave it another go.

This book explores the idea of getting on board a *waka*, a traditional carved Māori canoe used by the *tipuna* (ancestors) to cross perilous seas to come to New Zealand/Aotearoa. Simple and effective, these boats made it across the Pacific against all odds. We like to think of ourselves on such a *waka*, rowing together across the ocean towards the full reality of the kingdom of God, a journey of adventure and calling. Though we are not sure what our destination will ultimately look like, we trust we will recognize it when we see it, finding it as we go, finding it as we row. There is rhythm in our movement, for if we are to sustain the journey, we have to work together. When the weather and conditions change, how will we keep going? How can we challenge our surrounding culture, that strong tidal drift that pulls us off the course of our good intentions, allowing us just to pick and choose a theology from the bits of the Bible which are safe or nice, keeping us comfortable, isolated and distracted? As we paddle against the tide, we watch the well-intentioned pulled and tossed this way and that. Sometimes we see folks give it a go only to fall out. We have fallen overboard ourselves.

It's not easy to get on a Jesus *waka*, but if we are keen to paddle against the strong cultural tide and keep going towards the kingdom, we will need to travel lightly. There will be some things we'll need to throw overboard, which will free up space so we can pack on the vital things we'll need to have for the adventure ahead.

As we travel, we discover there is a whole fleet of boats out there on the water, each traveling in the same direction, each finding the same destination as they go. Each boat has a different design, each crew a different rowing rhythm.

But look in the water—there are people drowning out there! You might be sinking yourself! So for the sake of his kingdom, for the sake of a struggling and broken world, for the sake of your own soul, get off the beach! Get out on the water! This is the life we are waiting for, the abundant life of the kingdom. You were made to row this canoe, so get on the *waka*!

PART ONE

Throwing It Overboard

ONE

Going Deep:
Throwing out the "Next" and the "New"

Over twenty years ago, after Justin and I got married, we lived above a community center in a poorer suburb of Wellington, a multicultural neighborhood with a variety of older housing and high-density council flats. As youth workers with teens from a variety of cultural backgrounds, we were perfectly situated on the main road, close to the bus stops, with a fish and chips and a pizza shop downstairs as well as a community space for club nights and bigger meals, where we could even sneak in some extra accommodation. Our place leaned a little, leaked a little, and was very noisy as it rattled with the passing traffic, but it was our home, which was what our young people needed. We had an open-door approach to our youth club, which meant our house was full of teenagers all the time. Whether sleeping on the couch, playing guitar on the steps, raiding the pantry or smoking in the doorway outside, they came to see us and to hang out with each other.

We made a conscious decision early on to do it this open-home way, knowing that for an average teenager, it wouldn't work to be available at certain times, but not at others. This didn't mean we didn't get tired: there were often late calls and visits all week long. But we learned to take our "time out" away from the house so that the door could remain open and the teenagers would always be welcome.

One late night, when we had been doing youth work for many years, Justin, along with a group of other community workers, were sitting round a small fire under the stars with one of our favorite mentors and friends, Charles Ringma, a theologian who has kept his feet on the ground, involved at the grassroots, on the margins, fully engaging even when working in prestigious positions. Charles's wife, Rita, is an artist who has shared her life, art, and studio with the poor rather than hiding away in a studio to express herself. When we feel like giving up, their lifestyle inspires us on again.

Looking round the circle, Justin took the opportunity to ask Charles: "If there was one piece of advice you would give to a young adult in their twenties, a young adult interested in following Jesus, what would it be?" Charles said that young adults need to find a cause worthy of their engagement and then pursue it with everything they have, going hard for it, pouring their lives out for their dream! What contrast to the constant warnings we'd heard against burn-out, towards boundaries and balance. How resourceful to use our young adult energy for the kingdom of God, to pour ourselves into the things God values!

Like most young adults, I remember that feeling of standing on the edge of a world of possibilities, the endless experiences ahead for me to taste and enjoy. I could not only see all there was to do, but could think up a million new ideas that hadn't yet been done. Because I had energy and a little talent, I probably could have done most of them: youth work, teaching in a poorer school, children's work, working with newly arrived refugee families, recycling and environmental projects, alternative cottage industries for working women in the sex trade, church work, worship team, drama group, overseas development work . . . my list went on and on.

But I knew I couldn't do all of them, so—because I loved teenagers— I made a choice to begin with Youth for Christ and got stuck in. I could have made another choice from my long list of dreams. It didn't matter so much what I chose but the fact that I chose something and got going. This is what made the difference for me, actually committing to something. Youth for Christ were welcoming of me, and the new faces and new ideas kept my interest high.

But when Justin and I had done youth work for a while, it wasn't new and it didn't seem so exciting any more. Many others came and went quickly. There were many other options to move on to, even within our YFC world. There were bands to play in, tours to go on, big shows to put on for thousands of kids. They drew the cool guys and lots of the talent. Consequently we found we weren't a team of the coolest, most onto it young adults. I wanted to jump so badly, but something stopped me.

You see, through our commitment to them, we had begun to love the young people in our neighborhood. As we invested in them, they invested in us. They were under our skin and in our heart. We began to want what was best for them, and we could sense God's call. Our club kids didn't connect to a church, and our ministry had little impact on anyone else in our wider Christian world at the time, but they had us and we had them and we began to go deep.

Meanwhile our church congregation began a big new community house in a huge old place with tons of character. Situated at the end of a long driveway, it was full of rooms and had a big lawn, perfect for events and parties. Weekends there were pumping with social life. Living in a big community house was a new idea for us back then, and they were buzzing about it, drawing a much cooler bunch than us—they were even written up in an American book on radical community. Eating chick peas and doing art, picnicking on the lawn and painting banners for social action, there was always a laugh to be had around the large dinner table. They were also giving some great hospitality to people who were really strug-gling, and our church was always buzzing about what they were doing.

We wanted to move over and be part of that group, on the hub of what was hot! We wanted those chick peas on our plate, that profile in the church, that sense of belonging to something that mattered. Yet we loved our young people, and we sensed God did, too, so we stayed faithful to our little team and kept going in our little house above the centre. We didn't know then that this choice to stay faithful to one dream was so radical, nor that it would be so pivotal for our longevity in community.

There will always be new ideas, new opportunities, the next great adventure, but we live in a society where the next and the new is way out of balance. In Robert Chamber's *Rural Poverty Unperceived,* he makes the point that if there was a malnourished child on the floor in the middle of our room, we would all take immediate action. We would feed the child, hug the child, clothe the child. Yet we know the world is full of children like this who need our support, and yet we do nothing. Why? Proximity. By allowing ourselves to go deep in one place, we bring ourselves into the proximity which demands our action.

Chambers also says that poverty is never found on the main road. Instead, poverty is on the back roads of our society. The more successful we are, the more options we have, the more we tend to stay on the main roads of our society. The more successful and talented we are, the harder it is for us to find the back roads of our society and the harder it is to stay there. Multi-talented people always have options and need a larger amount of self-discipline and faithfulness. Perhaps that's what God meant by, "To whom much is given, much is expected."

Our Western affluence adds options to our lives. I compare the passion I see in New Zealand youth workers to that I have seen in Cambodian young adults involved with TASK, the NGO Servants have set up in Phnom Penn. I had the privilege of meeting with TASK young adults who talked to us about their work in the slums, educating their peers in issues of sexual health and wholeness. They were so passionate that their faces literally shone. They loved their work with the young people; they loved talking about it with us. For them this opportunity had added such value and meaning to their lives. They loved their calling; they loved their belonging; they even loved the team T-shirt! There was a passion in them I struggle to find in New Zealand youth workers. So often in New Zealand we are so ho-hum about our involvements. We might do a little of it for a while and then again we might do something of the other hundreds of options in our lives. Guess which team finds their work more fulfilling?

Our decision to do one thing well affected our approach to youth work. We moved from a program-based approach to a sharing-all-of-our-lives approach. The space of belonging we created as a team was all about and all for our young people. For us this kind of thinking marked the start of a holistic lifestyle. We began to live with an open door, eating together, working together, living together. Even supermarket shopping would usually have some teenagers in tow. It wasn't about doing a program, it wasn't about providing a service, it was about sharing life and making friendship.

In fact our summer job in those years was working with the city council's Summer City program, running recreation programs on beaches and in parks over the summer months. We could have kept this work to the side of our lives, but that would have meant hours away from our neighborhood. Instead we decided to employ our young people and leaders to work alongside us on the beach, painting kids faces and running games for families. There were liabilities, of course, when the large bear suddenly rips off his head for a cigarette, or the kids' castle is suddenly left unattended while someone sneaks off after their girlfriend. It was extra effort on one level to keep it good with our boss and safe for the public, but it was worth it. Working together was important to our belonging. It allowed more of life to connect. Giving kids real skills for employment felt more valuable than another car rally. It was potentially professionally damaging, but it took us deeper with the kids.

This invitation to depth is important to the work God does in each season. First, for the sake of those we serve and love. For us in our early years, it was our young people. We loved them enough that we couldn't just add a whole lot of other stuff to our lives and also have a life-changing relationship with them. We saw their lives change, and it wouldn't have happened with a half-hearted approach. They wouldn't have been cared for well, they would have missed out yet again.

Second, we couldn't learn what God had to teach us in that season if we hadn't gone deeply with this invitation. Though there often comes a time to move on (as Justin and I have since moved on), we have come to think of our lives in seasons of at least five years. Each season of involvement has had such significant learning and growth for us: skills, theology, self-awareness. We couldn't have matured in these ways by staying on the edge, by being too busy, or by always moving on to the next best thing. We have always hoped for God to help us change and we have only experienced it in the places where we have been committed deeply.

I think too that although we have learned so much on the way and are now far more skilled in what we offer, the raw commitment and energy we gave that first few seasons meant that it was possibly the best loving we ever did. In one way, it didn't ever get better than that. We were committed and going forward, and while we didn't know much, our young people knew we were all about them. I encourage young adults new to the journey to keep going hard for the people in pain whom they have come to love. I reassure them that they will grow and mature, but the passion of those young adult years can be the most amazing raw love.

When we talk about going deep and not wide, we often use the analogy of a romantic relationship. There is so much we can enjoy when we start going out with someone early on and, let's be honest, it's exciting. In fact, some people stay at that level of relating all their life. But only in making the commitment to the other do we really find that depth of relationship, that deeper knowledge, the real growth. All of our great lessons in life have come through commitment.

To find that life-changing passion with others, we have to go deep! We have to throw away the next and the new and grab hold of a dream and die for it.

DON'T MISS THE POINT

- Find an invitation within God's kingdom and give yourself totally to it for a season.

LOOK INTO IT

Matthew 13:44–46
Ask yourself: Have you found your pearl? Have you paid the price?

TWO

Staying Faithful:
Throwing out Experience Seeking

In my family, an overseas trip was a rite of passage, along with tertiary education. The day my older brother left on the plane to explore the world, we gathered round him at the airport, and I knew that soon, my time would come. It felt like my right to get on that plane and leave all my responsibilities behind, to consume the world's adventures. My siblings were based in London, and their letters and calls home were full of their latest trips all over Europe, exotic people, places, food, ideas, and experiences. My parents had tales from their travel days, and they were proud of my siblings' adventures. Justin's parent's had travelled, too, as had his brother, offering us exotic Asian connections to pick up on.

So when Justin and I finished our study, we had to decide whether or not we were prepared to surrender our "right" to travel. This was our time, our rite of passage. We needed a few years to go and experience the world, didn't we? But what about our calling to our young people? If we left when we wanted to, there would be no one to take over the work. And we couldn't just replace ourselves, because that's not how friendship works.

Around this time I remember a young woman arriving late one night in an agitated state. She had just finished her school exams and didn't feel like she had done so well. She was tired and angry and she'd come to crash on the couch for the night. But as the night wore on she started unloading the real pain of her year. Unknown to her family and us, she had become pregnant that year and had lost the baby. The relationship

9

had then finished, and she had been left burdened and broken hearted. As she talked and cried with me, she shed a load she had carried alone.

Right there on our couch, I had the privilege of reassuring her of God's love for her, of holding her when she asked me to call her parents and invite them round, of watching her be honest with her dad, of watching him cry and hold her and then take her home. Being there over time, in committed friendship, meant I could love her as God loved her—when it really counted. I knew I wanted to be present for this young woman and others like her. These people were my priority, and focusing on earning enough for my OE would have pulled me away from them.

Soon after we made the decision not to take the OE, we were given the gift through my studies of round-the-world tickets. On the one hand, we still wanted to experience the world, but what would happen to our young people? How would we continue to provide the safe space they needed? They needed our couch! They needed us to help them debrief their bad days and make good choices. They needed to know their value within God's family.

In the end, we chose to go, but only for six weeks. We felt that if we left for longer, we would risk losing what we had with our club kids. When we left, our club kids all came to the airport (during school time, I'm afraid) with guitars and food. We had a sing, a feed and big hugs goodbye. And while away we wrote to them, kept in good touch, collected little gifts and actually couldn't wait to get back to them all. Even though we had a great trip with my teacher-college friends, visiting castles and climbing mountains and meeting great people, it didn't compare to the depth of our life back at home in our neighborhood. It didn't compare to late nights on our couch. Our love for them by now was far greater than our love for the new experience.

Even though we surrendered our "right" to the OE, it didn't mean that the love of travel had gone away. But when God graciously gave us back opportunities to travel, they aligned with our commitment to the people around us. With the girls from Te Whare, we got to travel to UNOH in Melbourne, where we fed the girls scary new foods, billeted them with families from different cultures, marched the streets for the closing of the casino, met Burmese refugee activists, and vomited together on roller coasters. In fact some of the girls who went on that trip remain my best friends. Afterwards, we were astounded to learn that the highlight for our girls was their engagement with the Burmese refugees, affirming that this deeper way to live is appealing to our young people, too, if we give them the chance.

Since then, many young adults in and around our community have had to answer the travel question, particularly as we have begun wrestling with the environmental impact of travel. Should we fly at all? Can we travel another way? Hitchhiking can add interest to a journey without adding carbon.

I have been impressed at how many have chosen to travel—or not—in line with their convictions and faith. Many have opted for slum retreats or mission conferences as opposed to backpacker fun times. Others have built a relationship with one place in the developing world or with a community working overseas (Servants, UNOH, Waiters, InnerChange). Some of our friends have gone to live overseas to be part of God's kingdom agenda in difficult places. Others have traveled when it worked for the people in their neighborhoods best, and they have cut trips shorter or taken others with them. Many have chosen each year to stay rather than go at all, and their neighborhoods have been blessed by their sacrifice.

Travel isn't the only thing that competes for our faithfulness, distracting us from the kingdom agenda of the lost and the least. New experiences are always on sale for those who can afford to consume them. When we are not traveling, we can still buy experiences from all over the world—whether it's our food, clothes, toys or adventures.

Even within the church, we love the new experiences. We love to rush over and be prayed for, to fall over laughing with the Spirit's power. It doesn't matter how late it goes or how far we have to drive, we're up for it. Justin calls it "Christian bungee jumping." But does all this experience-seeking mean that our ministry to the poor becomes more powerful and our spiritual lives more mature? Not usually.

For me it has been helpful to accept that I will never do everything, see everything, or meet everyone. Jesus did not seek after events or experiences, but people. Accepting the calling I have with gratitude helps me struggle against the tide of experience seeking.

Don't Miss the Point

- God's invitation is full of wonderful adventure and experiences. He offers us abundant life!

- The challenge is to live fully the experiences that come out of our involvement, not to seek experiences as goals in themselves.

Look Into it

Mark 8:34–37
Ask yourself: Do you seek experience or live a life of calling?

THREE

Living the Dream:
Throwing out Entertainment

While visiting the UK last year, our family had the privilege of being part of the Lifeline Expedition, a team of folks who walked around the trail of slave history—through Africa, the Caribbean, and across the UK—over a seven-year period. The teams, comprised of both slave descendants and slave-trader descendents, walked, ate, and prayed together over the journey, but this time, the white people wore shackles. Journeying through each town, the team retold the story of slavery in that particular place and invited both people of power (mayors, community leaders, ministers . . .) and ordinary folk to respond. Some wept, some apologized, and some extended forgiveness, drawing many towards healing and reconciliation.

Justin and the kids joined the team between Birmingham and Liverpool, and Justin said it was incredibly uncomfortable to walk in the shackles with his children tied to him—both emotionally and physically. As they walked, extreme white-power groups abused and threatened the team for "enticing white guilt."

After our return from the UK, we were inspired to learn more about the Clapham Sect, a small group of Christians led by William Wilberforce, who confronted the English government with the hideous realities of the cruel deaths and torturous lives these stolen slaves suffered for the profit of the English merchants. Challenging the parliament towards justice, they lobbied, protested, raised awareness, and rallied support for the abolition of slavery.

After nearly a decade, they had converted enough members of parliament to bring in the bill that would lead to the abolition of the slave trade. Imagine their excitement and relief—justice was just round the corner!

But on the very same night, as parliament sat with that particular bill, a new show opened on the West End, London's fashionable theatre district. It was usual for politicians of the day to keep up with new shows, because people noticed who was there and that was important. Assuming others would attend the parliament session, different individuals took the opportunity to be the first to see the new show. And so, tragically, the bill did not pass, and it took another eleven years to have the numbers of votes needed to pass the bill again. That meant one million more people were moved from their homes and families in Africa to a life of abuse and slavery in the UK.

What were those politicians thinking? How could they have missed that vote? They were out there entertaining themselves, leaving others to be abused and killed. What sort of culture allows such priorities? How badly history now reads them.

For Wilberforce and his friends, this was not a one month or one year campaign, but a faithful calling they followed for forty-six years. We struggle to commit for one year! How will history read us? Are we out there entertaining ourselves while the world is starving and dying? Could our culture have an entertainment addiction that takes priority over everything else?

We have talked already about the tide of overseas experience, of moving about from one thing to the next, but if we are staying put in one place, how do we cope with the entertainment all around us? How do we keep ourselves from being distracted by a hundred pointless journeys here at home?

Now I love movies—love jumping into a new world through cinema. With limited time and money, it doesn't happen often, but when a precious opportunity comes, I stand at the board outside the box office staring up paralyzed, promising myself that if I hurry up and make one choice today I will make sure that I get back to do the next one soon.

Then there are the books I could read, the community night classes I could take, the social running events I could train for (believe me they would take a lot more time to have a shot of getting me over a finishing line), the tramping I always imagine, the art projects I am halfway through.

And then there are all the new cafés, the scent of roasting coffee sweeping into the street, calling "try me!" And inside each café, full of new styles and new colors, there are such cool looking people to stare at, piles of papers and magazines to read, new sounds to listen to—and that's before I even look at the menu and see all the new names and new flavors.

From one who can pack a lot into life, I find entertainment exhausting! And that's the problem; it exhausts us of our time, our money, our energy, and our focus, distracting us from the reality of what's happening in our lives and in our neighborhoods. And who misses out at the end of an action-packed week? The same people who always miss out, those in our neighborhoods who are lost and lonely. The fact may be that they may be entertaining themselves in their little council flat, chocker full of blackware (TVs, DVD players, etc.). But distracting ourselves isn't offering them the alternative they need.

Most of what we do to entertain ourselves may seem harmless in itself, although a scratch under the surface of the movie, music, food, and fashion industries should give us all a hard slap. They are huge building blocks in the consumerist empire that is killing our planet, abusing the poor, and destroying our souls. Make the links for yourself between entertainment and advertising, between consuming and entertainment, between our entertainment industry and the poor, between our entertainment and our lust and greed. Even our youth work and our community work is often entertainment based. Can we be brave enough to admit that entertainment is idolatrous in our culture? And that it's killing us?

The good news, as always, lies in the fact that we have the imaginations to create an alternative. What if recreation in its purest sense is actually about re-creating, bringing life, not sucking it in? What if we were far more disciplined and thoughtful about our recreation choices so as to add to our inner resources rather than replete them?

Let's slow down a little and ask ourselves some questions: Does this movie inspire me, stir my compassion, add to my understanding of others in need? Does this book help me get to where I'm wanting to head? Could I spend an afternoon doing some art or gardening or walking somewhere beautiful rather than overloading my senses with this movie, this computer game, other people's messages for me. Is there a cheaper way to do this? A free way to do this?

I have a friend who inspires me with her wonderful garden, her homemade soaps, her house full of beautiful natural things, none bought from a city shop. When we meet for coffee, she brings the thermos, and we sit at the beach rather than in the café.

Then we can ask, how can we use our recreation, even our entertainment, to build the kingdom in our neighborhoods? If we are going out, why not invite those who don't get invited out? If we are staying in to a good movie, why not include those otherwise stuck at home with their own TV for company?

Recently we were reminiscing with some of our old girls from Te Whare Atawhai (who are now as old as we were then, how did that happen?). As we watched shaky amateur footage of roller skating, sing a-longs, parties, dinners, and dress-ups, one of the old girls commented, "There was always something going on." Not expensive or even cool (which is hard to admit) but just fun times to fill otherwise painful lives with good memories. Not only can we fill the void of meaninglessness with something healthy and creative for others and for ourselves, we can create a stock of good memories for the future.

One picture of this has been our Urban Vision musicals—first Joseph and then Jesus Christ Superstar. Set in Cuba Street Wellington, full of punks and prostitutes, our own neighborhood, we pulled off the shows to full and responsive audiences. The fact that disabled and less-able actors were included was all part of the magic of it—as was the fact that we were able to use this as a fundraiser for the children of Iraq.

A few years later, during a church service in the middle of the city, a friend from the neighborhood offered to share his life story. He took it very seriously and came in carrying large boards of photos. His eyes lit up as he explained his display: a few photos of him as a child and the rest were all of him as a soldier in our production of Jesus Christ Superstar!

More recently, we created a colorful rendition of Oliver Twist, with the majority of the cast our neighbors' kids and our own. Not once were the same group of kids at a rehearsal; Bill Sikes left in the middle of the night and had to be replaced; kids threw up and got injured; backstage was as entertaining as out front! But the money we raised helped Partners work with the kids of Myanmar, and the kids at the council flats talked about the show for the rest of the summer and keep asking when the next one will be.

Through plays such as these, kids are learning how to recreate well and to turn off the play station and TV. This kind of recreation brings life to the people who need it, helping them develop their talents, encouraging them to work on something even when it gets hard, and inviting them to belong to something and contribute.

Whether it's sport, drama, music, art, or fundraising, let's find the talent in our neighborhood and transform our entertainment-based culture into one that gives us all life and purpose.

Don't Miss the Point

- Recreation is vital to our health and well being.

- We are addicted to entertainment and it is drowning many in our culture.

- We have choices, and with some imagination our recreation can bring life, not destroy it.

Look Into It

John 10:10
Ask yourself: Do you recreate or do you entertain yourself? What is the difference? How does your recreation bring life to you and others?

FOUR

Finding Our Vocation:
Throwing out Career

As a young teacher, I was enthusiastic in my training. I took way more than the minimum credits and wrote extra varsity papers to add to my theoretical knowledge. Upon graduation, I looked forward to setting up my classroom. I wanted to be a good teacher partly because I cared for kids and wanted to help them learn, but I also loved having a profession to belong to, the status and challenge of a pay scale up ahead. Teaching was a respectable career: my parents approved, our government approved, society at large approved.

But I didn't know how to make this fit with Justin and my other life in our neighborhood. This wasn't straight forward for me. Upon graduating, there were no permanent positions in our neighborhood schools. My lecturers were encouraging me to accept any position offered, even if it meant relocating. I watched many of my fellow students relocate and shift into other areas, feeling great as they secured jobs. I, on the other hand, wasn't looking very successful. I had nothing in view and began to panic. Should we leave our community relationships to start again? Should I put my career on hold for a few years and risk looking unemployable at the end of it?

Finally, I was offered a relieving position in a local school, and I took it, even though I knew that wasn't a sensible way to start my career. But for us, staying in the neighborhood was a priority.

I knew this first job was an answer to prayer, but what about when it finished? I didn't like not knowing, and I didn't like not being in control.

Teacher's college lecturers didn't understand my choices, nor my fellow students, but I knew in my guts I had done the right thing. Even though I believed that God would bless my commitment to love both my teaching work and our neighborhood, many times I was tempted to panic and take a permanent job elsewhere.

At the end of the year, I found a part-time job teaching children with special needs in a school that was a two-minute walk from our home. I got on with the staff, and I knew all the families from my neighborhood. Even now when I walk round that neighborhood I have chats with former students and their families. Through this season, I began to see how God's plans were better than mine, if only I could conquer the stress of faith required in each step, something I still struggle with, nearly twenty years later.

But working part-time, I wasn't sure how I would finish my registration requirements. Yet when I looked into it, I found out it was possible to register part-time, even though my lecturers didn't recommend it. At the local school I was part of a vibrant team who got to know me, my family, and others who were working with us in the neighborhood.

When some other young teachers in our community graduated, we decided to apply for a job share together, though we had been warned that schools don't like job shares, especially between three people. But we applied, stating the benefits we could offer as a team. And the school loved the idea and were happy to give us a chance, because they knew us by then and knew we were committed to the kids in our neighborhood.

We had also been warned that teachers should maintain professional distance from their students. But we ran an after school club on Fridays, where we then would take the kids home and chat with their parents. We took families away on holiday and shared meals and cups of teas (and the best samosas you have ever tasted). In spite of all that, my reference from that season of my teaching never fails to pick me up a job these days. Though I have never become a senior teacher or added to my post-grad study—and maybe I never will—my teaching has been a part of my vocation, and not just when I am in the classroom. By thinking creatively, we imagined a different way to do things within the "system." It might be scary to push against these boundaries, but it's possible—and I am sure this is true in many fields.

Teaching may seem an obvious fit for community work, but the kingdom is broad, and over the years young adults in our community have had many career paths that have been carefully molded into their vocation.

Take Fiona, who ran our girls home, while also managing a career in the government, working herself up to a high position in the minister's office. Though she wore a suit sometimes, she dressed "down with the youth" at other times. Sometimes she had to be away from the home for a few nights, and other times she had to negotiate time off work to go to the police station, the principal's office, or the hospital. But the day she worked with a young person asleep under her desk at work, her colleagues became interested in her life. Her work with the girls did affect the jobs she accepted, the way she approached her government position, and the promotion she sought. How refreshing! I so often feel depressed when I hear people taking promotion, relocation, or extra work commitments without any sense of calling from God, without any sort of reflection about the consequences of such a decision. But Fiona loved her career and her involvement with the girls and was prepared to be a radical witness of God's love in both places.

Other professionals in our community have also found colleagues offering clothing, food, money, job experiences, and all sort of things to our friends from the neighborhood. So many people want to get involved, but they don't know how. Our approach to career doesn't only free up time for those who are struggling, it allows alternatives to become visible for those who are watching. It allows conversation to occur when people see us walking the talk of the gospel.

Another friend, Matt, was offered a position down at parliament after graduating, a great opportunity to get his career started. Yet he had dreamt about starting a business that married his love of coffee with his interest in fair trade and organics. The surrounding culture did not usher him in this direction, but he took the risk and the People's Coffee is now an exciting part of the Newtown team and has a good impact in the neighborhood and in the wider world of coffee. Right in the heart of the neighborhood where they live, there is always good coffee and conversation. Cafés all over their neighborhood—and even up the coast—have chosen to buy his fair-trade blends.

Matt has also gone on to employ people in the neighborhood and speaks to groups about justice in business. He has helped other coffee businesses get off the ground with roasting fair trade (certainly not the usual approach to business competitors). Matt is not following the dream of making the largest profit, but following a kingdom dream and making it a reality.

But it's not always as easy to find our dream and make it happen. Sometimes we just need to find some money to survive on. We juggle the principles of doing whatever it takes to get by and get the bills paid in order to participate in our part in God's kingdom with a refusal to waste our lives endlessly in jobs and careers that suck out our souls. We aim for a high percentage, a high proportion on the meaningful, "I just love this," part of our working lives, with a small proportion of "this is just what it takes" to keep us humble.

If we were to believe that "we are what we do," then most of us within Urban Vision would feel very inadequate. Luckily we believe that we are what God has created, and that we mature through our sacrifice and commitment. That doesn't stop the pressure of our families and peers, the force of the media. We still get tempted at times by the great professional ladders that we are falling off, particularly as we get older, since it gets harder. Our career options have decreased, our earnings have decreased, and our status in popular culture is low.

Justin remembers when two guys from our earlier youth work days coincidently visited on the same day. One of the guys had begun some study while he was living with us at the community center, but his schooling had been patchy and reading was a real challenge for him. We would come into the dining room some mornings to find the windows steamed up, heater still on and him asleep on the table with his head on his books. As they sat at the table having a cup of tea, he told Justin that he'd gone on to finish a degree and become a teacher. A miracle!

The second guy had also been part of that early team and had worked as a banker. As we got to know him we realized his day job was slowly destroying him. He didn't feel a sense of congruity to his values, didn't feel it was a match for his gifts and skills. It was a steady income, reliable, with a clear path of promotion (and pressure) ahead, but it had a high price on his soul. Through his time with us, he made the bold decision to resign and do a degree in theology. He loved Scripture and wanted to be useful to God's kingdom in a way that suited who he was. He went on to work as a pastor and chaplain in churches as well as prisons and schools.

As Justin heard these stories, instead of feeling a share in their joy, he felt surprisingly flat. In comparison, he felt left behind in the job market. Suddenly years of youth work and training seemed duller. Though these young men were reassuring of Justin's part in their vocational direction, he felt the cost of his choices.

Alone later, he prayed through his sense of rejection and failure in the world of career. He searched honestly for the voice of truth. When it came, he heard the voice of God's Spirit question him. Isn't this the point? Isn't it a great thing to become less so others can become more? He felt convicted. Of course this was the simple truth.

In fact, we are grateful that Justin has gone on to have many opportunities in paid work that have suited and stimulated him. But for our movement to grow and for our neighborhoods to find transformation, this sacrifice of status and security has been an ongoing price that many in our community have paid.

Even though many within Urban Vision have surrendered the right to a high-powered, high-paid, or high-status career, God has been faithful to us. He has provided for us in ridiculous and creative ways. We now have artists, teachers, HR folk, medical professionals, designers, engineers, policy analysts, lawyers, café workers, business people, trainers, factory workers, parents, retailers, youth workers, social workers . . . you name it. We have endless stories of great jobs that come our way that marry well our life in the neighborhood.

Many of us choose part-time work in order to free up time which we have come to see as our most precious resource. We realized some time ago that you don't actually have to work the forty-hour week year in, year out. There are other ways we can creatively imagine working life, we just have to risk security and stability to make it happen.

As a movement, we have been committed to being bi-vocational, earning our way rather than living on church support. That is not to say that churches haven't been very supportive of us at times. But we want a model which is more transferable to others, a model which most people can opt into. This allows the resources that the church does have to go a bit further, hopefully out of the West. And it requires a level of faith in us that we struggle and aspire to. We need God to help us make it work and to find ways for us to live cheaply. We need God to provide for us life-giving vocation.

Don't Miss the Point

- Sacrifice your career potential to build a vocation.

- Downward mobility may be the direction of God's call in your life.

- The big working machine has a lot more flexibility than you think.

Look Into It

Mark 1:14–20
Ask yourself: What has it meant for you to leave your boats and nets?

FIVE

Trusting God:
Throwing out Financial Security

When Justin and I were in our early youth-work days, we invited a couple of new friends, Māori youth workers from up the line, to come live with us, study in Wellington, and help with our club work. We'd visited their town on the East Coast a few times with our club kids. Think kids on horseback riding in the early morning mist, out to help milk on the farms. Think Māori being spoken fluently by everyone, not just students from the university. We weren't sure if they knew what they were getting themselves into, coming to live with a couple of Pākehā in the middle of a concrete jungle, but our young people loved them and we knew they could offer us much for our bi-cultural journey, Māori and Pākehā alike.

When their student allowance was slow to kick in, they couldn't pay rent. But this didn't matter much since Justin and I had saved two thousand dollars over the summer that we were happy to share. So we had club kids over and fed our guests, drove a beat-up old van for club, and still managed to pay rent. But the van needed petrol and maintenance, teenagers eat lots, and youth workers from up north eat more, so our hard-earned savings didn't last long, and we were going backwards rapidly.

We didn't want to stop what we were doing, so we went to those older and wiser and asked for advice. We chose people who knew us and loved mission and explained our financial situation and our dream. Some of our leaders strongly urged us to pull back from our involvement and get well paid jobs, to establish a financial base we could rely on for our future. They thought it irresponsible to continue and not to use our God-given talents to make money for our own keep. But our director at YFC took another approach. He simply said we should faithfully do what we knew God was calling us to and allow God to provide. We took his advice.

We continued to share life, give hospitality, and work part-time in the jobs we felt right about as part of God's plan for us. It wasn't laziness or trying to look radical or being anti- anything, but it was our passion for our young people. By the end of the year we had more in our savings than before. Without promoting ourselves, people had given us gifts, and we had learned how to live on less.

This was not easy. Rolled oats to fill out pasta dishes are not quite as nice; worse are the lentils we have come to eat as a staple. In big and small ways, we had to pull our weight in this miracle, taking on as much responsibility as we could, becoming far more disciplined with the little money we had.

Later, when we were in the inner city, we needed to draw again on faith in God as our provider. Initially when we moved down to the city, the offices of the Baptist soup kitchen were the perfect landing, but as others came, including a new baby to join our growing family, things were unbearable. We badly needed a bigger house for our hospitality, but the price was well out of our range. At this time Justin's work was ad hoc and I was only teaching a day a week. We felt God was walking ahead of us, encouraging us to take the bigger house, even though we didn't know how to make it sustainable.

Then Justin found a regular part-time teaching job, which was amazingly low on expectations outside class time. This allowed us to continue our main focus with the neighborhood and pay our extra rent. We also received unexpected support from a former leader in YFC who had heard about our work in the inner city and wanted to help out. Just when we needed God to provide, he did.

Then when we had a dream for some land to connect with our inner city involvement, we prayed for more faith and eventually found Ngatiawa, a perfect piece of paradise which had belonged to the Presbyterians, who were keen for us to purchase it and keep the spirit of their place going. Sensing God was in this, we left the city and we headed up toward the new land. The new team was ready to take over our place in town, and we were able to borrow a barn on a neighbor's farm while we sorted things out for the land sale. It was a little crowded with our three kids and two teenage foster girls, and there was only one light bulb in the middle of the room, but early nights were welcome after the late-night inner city lifestyle. And chatting to the older girls at night in the dark had a certain magic and allowed little ones to be asleep on time. It was like a really fun camp out for the first week or so.

But even though we had a good deposit, I had a part-time job, and Justin would soon have work up the coast, the banks didn't think we had enough income or security. After numerous banks declined us and our confident mortgage broker deserted us, we prayed, I cried, the camp out wasn't such fun, and we prayed some more.

At the same time, though we had agreed to offer some training to a YFC team in New Plymouth, I did not want to go. A long drive with all the kids was not the break I was looking for, and surely our friends there would understand that we were in the middle of a major crisis. But we sensed God encouraging us to honor this commitment, and so we went. As we unloaded our grief over strong cups of tea, our friend suggested a sympathetic banker in the small regional bank who had helped them buy their community house, even though he hadn't looked good for a mortgage.

As we had no home, all our paperwork was in the van, so between training sessions, we had an unscheduled mortgage meeting and came home having arranged a mortgage. Our lovely mortgage broker said she would take the risk as long as we promised to pay it back and that we never asked to borrow another cent! We kept our first promise.

When we arrived on our new land, we got busy scrubbing out the old hall for a new community space. The ugly electric heaters were the first to get ripped out, an easy task midsummer. But then it got cold. Ngatiawa is at the foot of the Tararua mountain ranges and "cold" is the just the beginning of winter. Think thick ice and deep frost on a sunny day. Of course we had no money left, but a supportive friend from the local parish offered to buy some fireplaces, which were installed on the second day of winter.

Now I'm not advocating rip and throw and wait for God to replace, but I am witnessing to God's faithfulness time and time again. We do our best (in fact we bust our guts) and pray in the rest (it even rhymes).

We have learnt to buy clothes at op shops, drive less, bike, walk and hitchhike more, share everything, eat less—both quantity and quality (less luxury food, particularly meat)—entertain ourselves and our neighbors for free or cheap, holiday where we are offered free places, or camp, and stop collecting bloody stuff we don't need! We have found it both liberating and challenging.

The challenge has been to stop comparing myself to my middle-class peers and to stop feeling a sense of self-righteousness at what I have sacrificed. If I try to stay mindful of my peers in the two-thirds world instead, I either feel completely overwhelmed or condemned for my greed and responsibility in trashing the planet. This draws me back to the grace of God, which helps me be gracious to my Western friends.

I like to keep in mind a visit to the Collin St. Baptist church in Melbourne, whose front door opens onto a central business district lined with designer stores and whose back alley is a gathering ground for heroin addiction. As we talked with them, they asked, "Who is the greater addict, the guy taking the fifty dollar hit or the lady buying the five hundred dollar handbag?" I am grateful for God's grace in helping me realize that my addictions as a middle-class consumer are exactly the same as my friends who are/have been addicted to alcohol, drugs, sex, and crime.

Will we choose to serve God or money? Both require everything. Tertullian wrote of the early Christian church, "they shared everything in common except for their wives!" We like that, and thinking of our resources as shared helps us stay grateful.

Unfortunately, the people often keenest to hear these messages are those who are irresponsible with money. For some, good news is learning to handle money wisely and to go get a job! We mustn't let this message fool us into being irresponsible or frivolous with money.

I'm talking more here about those of us who like to control our own lives and future in a way where we actually don't need God at all, where we will participate in the kingdom as long as it all fits comfortably within our means. We will follow God once we have our investments secured, offering him the change from our purchases and sharing what we have with the people we like.

What about calling, obedience, and faith? Let's get these words back into our everyday dialogue and maybe more soul-destroyed middle-class friends living in bland land may want to listen. It certainly means we can offer more to those who are struggling and need it most.

DON'T MISS THE POINT

- Allow God to guide and provide.

- Find a call and follow it obediently, developing the gift of faith.

- Make the commitment to a simple lifestyle and save your soul, your neighbors and the planet.

LOOK INTO IT

Luke 6:24 and Matthew 6:24
Ask yourself: What would it take for you to ensure you serve Jesus not mammon?

SIX

Nurturing Healthy Relationships:
Throwing out the Hollywood Romance

Early on, Justin met a young woman through theatre work and found himself falling for her, performing his best for her. She admired his talent, laughed at his jokes, and her intellect was sharp enough to challenge him. When they began seeing more of each other, he could hardly believe his luck in finding someone so smart, talented, and good looking.

But she didn't share his commitment to Jesus, and faith had little in common with her world view. The relationships he admired didn't have this kind of gap, yet surely his good feelings about her couldn't be wrong. Surely they could find common ground.

As he began to question the priorities he had held so strongly, his passion for the gospel life began to fade. He could see more clearly the hypocrisy of the church and had all sorts of reasons why the life of Christ wasn't that great after all.

Fortunately Justin had the gift of a deep conviction for his age and a stronger thinking rather than feeling base in operation, and so he decided that he couldn't surrender his passion for a radical Jesus life for this relationship. When we met, our passions were in common, and he tells others how glad he was to have waited for the deeper match.

Since then, we have watched many young adults move through this cycle, but finding a good match in partnership is only one of the many challenges we face in the arena of romance. The constant scripts of the ideal Hollywood romance leave us hankering for the hot, steamy, and romantic. This idea of an exciting new relationship rolls over and over our TV screens, ads, movies, and even in quality literature. It's a lot less entertaining to explore themes of older relationships once the fun and passion has settled a bit, once some of the challenges of longevity and depth kick in. Yet this pull is unanalyzed by most young adults.

Getting some health in this area early on is vital to our emotional health, to the love we offer other friends and neighbors, to our chance at healthy long-term marriages. It's also vital to the call of celibacy, which is a radical, faithful, and rare gift some of our friends offer the world.

But exploring partnership well is not easy. Let me create a typical scenario we experience within Urban Vision. I am offering a hypothetical story because I don't want to connect this to one particular person.

She meets him at the annual hui (gathering). He's funny and so kind to the young boys he looks after. Obviously he's strong in his faith, or he wouldn't be there. He notices her on the second night, and they have a chat over tea.

At a meeting the next day, the group is looking for people to organize the end of year reflection service. She sees his hand go up and he looks in her direction. Her hand goes up too. Now there will be meetings together, and he will see her creativity.

Her friends have noticed, and they all stay up late, drinking tea, and talking about guys. So often she has had nothing to add, but now she has something to say. Although she only has a vague frame of who this guy is, she begins to fill him in from her wish list, assuming the best all the way.

During the meetings that follow, they find themselves sitting together and having another coffee afterwards. This isn't great for her study, but its only this once ... or twice ... well, now that it's regular, she didn't care that much about passing her course anyway. Besides, she can make up study time in the weekend because the others can take the girls out without her. After all, she's not paid to be here. They can't expect too much. This relationship is important, and she can't be expected to get to know him with others around.

Soon they're going out, something she feels hesitant to mention to her mentor, though she's unsure why. Yes, it's a bit fast to be going out. Yes, he's just arrived in the community, so no one really knows him, but she knows him. He's different. And she was still feeling so bad about the last relationship, which left her a bit messy. That wound is finally feeling in the background now. Maybe the eating thing will get better now too. She does want to keep the weight off, but she hates herself less at the moment. He makes her feel good again.

Yes, she is praying about it. In fact she is begging God for it to be right this time. She tells her parents, who are always keen for her to meet someone. Her sister was married young, and they are suspicious of the whole community thing, but going out with a young man, well, that's normal. They are stoked.

Summer gives a chance to go on holiday. It's clear for her from her family evangelical background that sex before marriage is wrong, well probably wrong, well maybe wrong, and who says the conservatives read the text right? But sharing a tent is not the same thing anyway. She hasn't eaten for weeks, and she has lost plenty of weight for the beach. Not like the younger girls who binge and throw up. They have eating disorders—hers isn't like that.

The summer holiday is hot, particularly inside the tent. Waking up in the morning, she feels a bit guilty. She didn't mean to get intimate so fast. He doesn't seem to be feeling so bad. In fact, he ignores her most of the day. Off with the guys. She feels a bit jealous. At night it's clear they are in love. Talking to him about her feelings, though, seems to suffocate him, and he seems to talk to her less these days.

She misses the girls and likes texting them. He seems less interested about his young guys. In fact he is talking about saving up for some travel next year. She's suddenly unsure if she's included in the plan.

Getting home to the girls is hard. She really just wants to be with him the whole time, yet when they're together it's not quite what she's hoped for. Who she hoped he'd be is substantially different from who he really is. They fight a lot over little things. But her close women friends and mentors have been pushed aside. Finally the bubble bursts.

If this sounds like an American teen novel, I can only sigh: welcome to our world. The scenario from here ends with one or both leaving the community. Or them getting engaged (help!). Or the longer, now far more complex, task of pulling things to pieces, working on her issues, his issues, their issues and rebuilding slowly in a far more disciplined way toward something that is stable, solid, and has the chance of going the distance.

Of course, this is a valuable process, but done badly it takes extra time and energy.

Maintaining a healthy partnership, even in marriage, is hard, but the better the foundation, the easier it is. Even then it's a matter of choice after choice to work, to commit, to stay with it. Sometimes something new and exciting feels just as tempting as it used to. But as we grow older in relationship, we continue to build on the discipline from our early years.

I live fully aware of the responsibility I have toward all the teenagers I have cared for and the friendships I have formed in my neighborhood. These folks rely on the stability and health of my marriage. Good news for them is seeing and connecting to a marriage that lasts, a marriage free of violence and abuse. The teenage girls benefited from experiencing a safe and healthy family environment. It allowed them to re-experience some positive family life and for some even offered tools in their own child raising. They need this alternative to hold. It is hope for them. If I were to screw it up now (literally), this would be incredibly selfish of me—not only for my own kids and Justin, but also for our older girls, because it would destroy their hope of an alternative.

I am blessed to have a partner who is respectful and caring, sharing the domestic load and the parenting, sharing life as my equal. This is a radical alternative to some guys out there in our neighborhood and offers hope to the women as well.

Doing a relationship badly, even early on, affects our team life too. Others can feel rejected and pushed out. Honest talking can stop. It is a constant area of fragility for us, but sharing our involvement is much more useful to assessing compatibility than intense coffee dates with a lot of "snogging." Sorting out our own issues does not slow up relational connection, but speeds things up, in a good way.

I also have stories of times when people have taken the time to do their own work first and have entered a relationship in good shape. They are then able to commit quickly or wait patiently for the right time, without throwing away the rest of their lives.

We have had relationships which have been done so well, and they have the added bonus of the community feeling so confident for them and really celebrating their commitment process without reserve. We have had couples who have shared their relationship with our young people and our neighbors. Engagements have been celebrated, weddings planned, including folks who don't often get invited to celebrations. For some of our young people it's been their first time in a bridal party, for others it's been their first time at a wedding. We have helped our neighbors and our young people as they have grown up to explore, commit, and celebrate their own partnerships. Talking through issues with young couples and those in our neighborhoods is some of the most satisfying chatting we do. Some of our neighbors are able to look at good partnerships in our community and begin to want it for themselves. Other neighbors feel supported by us in their values of faithful commitment, and we can help them stick together. We can normalize monogamy and celibacy.

Others too have explored relationships carefully allowing a change of heart without damage. How much better it is to leave a relationship without needing months of counseling. How much better it is to decide I'm not ready or this isn't quite right for me without the guilt of leaving someone trashed.

Self-discipline is a strength, a gift we give ourselves by avoiding pain and emotional damage. We also offer this gift to our partners. Justin held self-discipline pretty highly in his relationship with me (much higher than me, I must admit). This allowed us time to be sure we were a good match. I now have the gift of being able to fully trust him to continue to be disciplined and therefore faithful to me, both in his actions and in his thought life. Otherwise I would have had to hope he could suddenly develop these characteristics later, in time to keep a long-term partnership together.

In terms of keeping our sexuality in a good proportion, I use the analogy of a good piece of cake. Sex and physical intimacy (have you heard the term technical virginity?) are like the butter. The process of actually making the cake is important. Then enjoy the whole cake, which includes plenty of butter, and that makes it delicious. Too many people just lick the butter and end up throwing up.

DON'T MISS THE POINT

- Relationships done well are a gift to everyone.

LOOK INTO IT

Luke 14:15–35

Ask yourself: How will you ensure your romantic relationship(s) don't exclude you from the banquet?

SEVEN

Opening Our Homes:
Throwing out the Picket Fence

Before I was married, I was living in a cool flat in Newtown, complete with rodents, musicians, filth, and far too many bodies on the couch. I knew it was cool because only cool people were allowed to move in. It was surprising to me that I had made it. I loved the student life and my new life as a youth worker. I was always busy—at church, teachers college, youth club, my part-time job, and now my really cool flat with others who were in a different social world.

But I wasn't sure how to keep all the groups happy. There were my family, school friends, workmates, flatmates, old friends, sports mates, church friends, those we did ministry with, and friends in our neighborhood. I wanted to care for everyone and worked hard spending my time between all these groups of people, but it was tiring. And at the end of a busy week, the folks who missed out were the ones in our neighborhood who were struggling. With only the leftover dregs of our lives to offer, they didn't get much.

Others were experiencing some of the same frustrations. Some of our club leaders weren't able to invite the kids home because their flatmates weren't willing to keep things appropriate. Others were missing prayer meetings or club nights as social events or church activities clashed.

And so, alongside our exploration of a physically simple life, we decided to explore a socially simple life, choosing to create community around our households. This meant the people we lived with were also the people we did ministry with, socialized with, and worshiped with. This left us far fewer people outside to connect with, making it suddenly much easier. We had to eat; now we ate with our young people and friends. We had to go shopping and do housework, more opportunity to communicate, hang out or at least save each other time. It was a simple move that changed our lives.

Setting up a community household wasn't always easy. Traps for new players included having some people in the house who were not really sharing the agenda. Their motivation was financial or social, but they weren't called to hospitality. Sometimes we were not clear enough at the beginning about exactly what the house's purpose was, so people moved in with one expectation, others had different expectations, and that caused massive tensions, which pulled us apart and took loads of energy to sort out.

We are much clearer these days and avoid filling an empty space rather than waiting for someone who is really onboard. We are not scared to make it clear what we're into. There are plenty of other flats and community houses round if someone is looking for something else. But we keep it focused on involvement in the neighborhood and good belonging together. We keep Jesus central too. Rhythms of prayer are as vital to our households as weekly shopping or dumpster diving.

And because those we knew who were struggling in our neighborhoods became our priorities, other things in our homes changed, too. It has meant being alcohol-free for the sake of those with drinking problems, pork-free for our Muslim neighbors, and having simple food for the sake of making a tight budget stretch.

When we moved into the inner city, finding a place took imagination, since the housing was so expensive. As Justin and I wandered round early on, praying and looking out for the spot to be, we finally narrowed it down to one block that had the kind of color we were drawn to: red light bars, tattoo shops, op shops, and cafes. Many of the folks in that area lived in clothing bins and on park benches, but that wouldn't work for us as a family.

Then, on one of our afternoon prayers walks, we came across the local Baptist church folks out painting the front of their building. We were pleased to make the connection, since they were working in the same area and offered shared meals, three lunchtimes a week. As we got chatting, they mentioned their office space upstairs. Our ears pricked up, and we innocently asked if we might have a little look. As we climbed the stairs Justin and I both knew in our guts this was the start.

There was no running hot water, no clear glass windows in the living space (meaning there was only a small amount of sun over the summer months and none for the rest of the year), no kitchen except in the community center downstairs (which made for a lot more shared meals if we forgot to lock the street door), and it only had three rooms plus a storage area. It also backed onto the fish factory, a twenty-four-hour operation that was noisy and stinky. Hardly what I had in mind when I thought about having a little family of my own (my kids' room was the length of one bed and the width of the other). But it was perfect, because it was the space that allowed us to live our dream.

Luckily, the Baptist church was willing to let a few of us (eight, in fact) move in "temporarily." (We were also fortunate that when this turned into eighteen months, our friendship with them survived.) But crossing a social norm and throwing out our rights to private space has been common within Urban Vision. Even when we found a bigger house, our friend Cat had to live on a shelf above the stairs, in which she could only kneel. Another friend created "the hatch exit" in a wall with no door, which allowed him to share his room modestly with Brenda. Sacha survived a damp internal room built in the corner of the church space for a while. Our girls' home workers always shared rooms with the teenagers. But it's not always been easy, especially in the middle of winter.

We've always followed a good sense of location rather than an available building, which has usually meant waiting a little longer for the right place. It has also meant moving a few times to work out the needs in a neighborhood or swapping rooms to get the right combination of people, accommodation for children, or a new couple keen to get involved. For some, this has meant shifting houses more than they would like. More than once, we have found that the right house in the perfect location already has other people living in it. So sometimes we've asked for other people's houses. And when they've said no, we've prayed, done some work to make another house work for them, and then asked again.

Even married couples joined in these creative arrangements. Usually after an initial time on their own, couples have been prepared to share a household with all sorts of others. And when kids have arrived, they, too, have enjoyed the life of a wider household. Not easy to explain to your mother-in-law why the precious grandchildren share their home with wayward teenagers or strange looking street people. Yes, there are safety issues, and we attend to these carefully, using all the wisdom and discernment God gives us. But life is risky, and rich and we don't want our kids to miss out on the color of God's kingdom.

In fact our children are amazing at hospitality. They have all grown up knowing that sharing your toys is good and sharing your home is too. We have worked hard to make this way of life work well for our children. We have talked and debated, brainstormed and shared ideas about how to involve our kids, protect our kids and grow our kids. I am convinced our community life has been a precious gift to them, and that they in turn have offered so much to our neighborhoods. We have young people who will say to us now that they would never have stayed with us through the rough times without our kids. It seems that little ones can express unconditional love in a way that is much easier to understand. Our kids don't see people in categories such as "addicts" or "homeless." They just learn people's name and get to know them. In fact, years after we arrived in the city, my son asked if we knew anyone who we would call "homeless," and when I gave him a long list of his friends he was quite surprised. He only knew them as friends.

In parenting in the neighborhood, I have realized how simple the best lessons of life are for all of us. Our kids have always understood that it is better to solve problems without hitting. So when they hear a fight outside they know others need to learn this too. They've always known that certain behavior results in "time out" and that adult time out is called "jail." They know people need love and if they don't get enough they end up trying to find love in all sorts of sad ways. And that poverty means people sell what they can to survive. There is nothing I have found that cannot be explained in a way children can understand without scaring them. They have a robust understanding both of how good and hard life is. We are careful not to overload them with the problems of the world.

We let them live their childhood full of freedom, fun, and play. But they serve with us and contribute so much. They are often a huge witness to the alternative of the kingdom, and people comment on the difference they see in all our families.

But it has always been important for us to establish homes that are warm and beautiful, not only for our hospitality and for our children, but for our own souls. When I've had the privilege of visiting the urban poor neighborhoods in Asia, I am always amazed at the creativity of these families to make home within the limits of their simple houses. In the midst of rubbish piles and hot stench, there are always those who are growing flower pots around their houses. They hang family photos and decorations on the walls and always make a welcoming space for visitors. They teach me that we don't have to spend heaps of money or buy heaps of stuff to make a home. Home and Garden magazines may not be the inspiration we follow, but we do put effort and resource into creating a haven. We've been blessed to have artists among us who create beauty, as well as orderly folks (although I have to say there are less of these in my world, why is that?) who set up the space to be functional for everyone.

Watching some of my peers go up and down emotionally with the market and spend all their spare time doing up houses and selling them, only to buy and start again, I'm so glad that the picket fence of our cultural dream fell down. Our expectation of a good family home, or the equivalent cool-student pad, depending on our age and stage, has had to be reviewed. But we are freer of that cultural pressure than we would have been. We're rowing against that tide.

Miraculously, many of us have bought land or property, but matching the location to the dream has always been the priority. We don't shift because of the market prices or the "potential, potential, potential" of a great little cottage. We have bought in together or shared our places (even if we end up feeling squashed) to make it work, and we have often heard criticism over our less than best financial management. Many of us have kept on renting, staying on in a place even when it leaks or is less cool than we would wish.

In the end, we can have a castle mentality about our homes, where we draw up the drawbridge and close out the wicked world. Or we can treat our houses as motels, which we check in and out of in between living a life out there. Or we can create a home that is a warm and safe offering we extend to others. Offering home in our modern world is one of the most radical things we can do. Not just Sunday lunch, but a place for others to share life with, which nurtures the reality of God's welcoming family. That's the heart of the gospel.

DON'T MISS THE POINT

- A home is not just a flat or a house.

- We can create our homes to nurture the dream and the people.

- We start with the dream and the best location for that dream, not with the most easily available place.

LOOK INTO IT

Luke 7:36–50
Ask yourself: What sort of hospitality will you show to Jesus? Do you have a home, a motel or a castle? Do you raise the drawbridge?

EIGHT

Paddling against the Current: Throwing out Respectability

Can you imagine the joy my mother felt when she knew that at twenty I was seeing a "nice young man"? Justin and I were serious, and the fact he didn't wear shoes, had something of an afro, and earned his money in odd ways was clearly just a student phase. After all, I, her own daughter, shopped at the op shop (second-hand store) in those days, dying old men's pajama pants purple, and shamelessly wearing them round the student world. (Incidentally, I no longer go for the old guys' PJ's these days after a bad incident involving unnoticed stains, but op shops are still mandatory on the budget.) Maybe she flinched a little when the wedding plans included loads of teenagers and was more down the cheap and inclusive end (stylish, of course, on a shoestring). Perhaps a bit more when our new little flat for the two of us soon became full of young people and other youth workers.

In fact, my father would joke with us in the 1970s that by the time we all grew up, my young girl's fantasy of marriage and family life would be obsolete and everyone would be involved in large group marriages living all together. (I would laugh in outrage, but now we nervously laugh at how close to the bone it really is!) At the point where I took the beautiful new grandchildren to live in a dodgy end of the city squashed into a dark office space with no hot water, she stepped back from thinking we were moving out of this phase.

Isn't it scary to think that God himself may actually have an invitation for our lives that may be different than the one our mothers always hoped for? That we may have a part to play in the story, the very same story that we read of in the Scriptures, which, let's face it, are a bit crazy. There were some pretty weird things that happened in those times to some otherwise normal, respectable types. Try telling your mother back then that you were ditching your work as a fisherman, the trade passed down from your dad and his dad, the job that brought in at least reliable money, for a new job—"fishing for people"—with no set income. A little harder to get your head round as a mother, I would think. Did Jesus' own family think he'd gone over a line the day they picked him up and he said, "who are my mother and brothers?" Jesus didn't go down as well as lots of our respectable Christian role models these days.

Looking less "successful" and at times a bit ridiculous has been challenging for all of us in Urban Vision. Losing the respect of others, especially our families and the friends we really care about, can hurt. Sometimes we find we are no longer well-heeled enough or successful enough to belong in certain circles. Sometimes these circles are inside our own families. We live in overcrowded homes, in hard-core neighborhoods, have odd people living with us, and pay to do it! "Shouldn't 'The Urban Vision' be paying you to live here?" say our concerned and indignant families. (Notice the "The" comes in at these moments, as if it is some institution with a pay clerk.)

Perhaps in the early days we ourselves thought of this kind of lifestyle as a season. Certainly each major life stage has required us to choose again, to set the agenda again. We realize that our own cultural norms pressure us each time, whether or not they are articulated by others. Now that I'm studying I need . . . Now that I'm married I need . . . Now that I have kids I need . . . There are real needs and adjustments that must be made at each stage of our lives, but how do we define these needs? How do we decide how best to live now? The answer for us has been to see our calling as lifelong, to follow Jesus to the margins. But each step on that track has looked different. We are imaginative enough, surely, to challenge pressure that comes from status, respect, or "normal" standards of living. Instead, we have established new ideas of "normal" and have offered one another understanding and respect based on kingdom values.

Unfortunately, our lives in radical community don't transfer into huge ups in the Christian world either. We don't even have too many tales of big revivals and huge conversions, for those whose concern could be eased by such statistics. The flavor of our community is often about sharing life, year after year, with people who find it hard to make positive changes. Their belonging to us simply helps them hang on, in all the trauma. Sure, we have precious stories of transformation in the lives of our neighbors and in our own lives. But these don't usually match up to the big expectation of "successful mission" and don't offer us positions of power or influence, even in the church.

Yet for some of us, it has been a blessing to watch family and friends take some of these wild new values on board. My own parents have had all manner of folk to their table year after year, including at special family times like Christmas. They cook for my friends, open their door, welcome others, and listen to their stories with interest. It has been life changing both ways.

In fact, I remember a time when Dad had come home from the supermarket. On observing a group of wayward looking youngsters loitering at the door he had initially felt nervous. You know those groups of kids wearing heavy black clothing in the middle of summer, smoking and swearing, looking out menacingly from under long greasy fringes. You hang on tight to your trolley and push past quickly. "But," he said, "I looked at them in the face and I thought any one of those girls could just be one of Jenny's girls." This was reassuring for him as he knew our girls not as societal problems but as individuals full of personality, potential, and sadness. Justin's parents too have embraced the madness. His mum was the favorite Grandma as she tucked boxes of cigarettes into our girls hands behind our back. In fact, at times I've had to pull Justin's dad back as he is inviting yet more crazy folk to join in on our family holiday.

Our families across Urban Vision have so often blown us away with their support. They have cooked at our gatherings, supported our recoveries, and often gotten involved in becoming the family which others were missing.

But for some among us, the rejection of others, including family and loved ones, the lack of understanding, and criticism, has been part of the high price to pay. The road of loving back in the face of this is not always easy. We have been surprised at the kingdom moments that have occurred even in the most hostile relationships, when the light goes on and people are able to see and share something of our hope and passion. But we always wish for more times like this.

I have to admit on a bad day I myself am known to groan, "Other women don't have to . . ." (feed this many people for dinner, go out and take someone to the hospital in the middle of the night, try to explain to my children's new friend's mother who the odd man is on the seat outside, etc.). Justin, being "slightly" less pastoral than me, rolls his eyes and asks when Jesus invited me to compare my life with others. In fact, such comparisons are a dangerous game. I suspect that this is the form of judging Jesus warns us to stay off. What if, instead, I were to compare myself with the mother I met in a Cambodian slum last year? Then instead of complaining I'd be paralyzed with guilt again. I have to say I was delighted recently when Justin, after rolling up his pants and taking his shoes off to cross the river at 6:30 AM in order to head into the city for work, moaned (with a twinkle in his eye), "Other men don't have to cross a freezing river to save ten bucks by hitching to work in the morning!" Sometimes we ourselves feel this pressure to conform; we feel the loss of our own respectability.

For many of us, St Francis has been one of our favorite mentors. He shunned the respect of others. At times when he felt others' admiration was in danger of pulling his devotion away from Jesus, he would run down the road in his undies or spend the day with brother Juniper on a see-saw, making a fool of himself for Christ. My nearly teenage family is probably less in favor of these methods for us at the moment, but we embrace the spirit of this man.

Perhaps in the name of being relevant and not putting people off, we are tempted to present the gospel as a mediocre tack on to the good life. But you cannot simply add the Jesus lifestyle on top of a normal, respectable lifestyle. It is not the nice extra to guarantee my ticket to heaven, to help ease my conscience, to enable me to get the best of all the worlds. The consumerist lifestyle is anti-gospel, for the gospel doesn't affirm cultural norms, but contradicts them. The gospel is offensive, and the lifestyle it calls us to lead will bring rejection and the loss of understanding, status, and respect.

Yet God calls us to be a peculiar people, a holy people. The hope we offer is in the alternative we live. Thankfully, we have the solidarity of each other on the journey and the love between us and the neighbors we serve. And we have Jesus, who knew all about it and paid a far greater price than we ever will.

Don't Miss the Point

- The pressure from family and friends to live in certain ways is very strong.

- Rejection and misunderstanding is part of the price of the gospel.

- God calls us to be a peculiar people.

- Following Jesus is not respectable.

Look Into It

Mathew 9:9–12 and Mark 3:31–35
Ask yourself: Who are you afraid of disappointing? How prepared are you to look foolish?

PART TWO

Taking It On

NINE

The Shared Life: Taking on All God Sends Us

When our little youth group tried to draw leaders from the church we struggled. We weren't new or cool, and we expected a high level of commitment to our young people. We wanted onto it leaders that would attract kids and make it more fun for us, but they were busy in the bands and on the stages of the church. So we made team with anyone prepared to show up regularly, who had the right attitude, and a love of the kids. Some of our leaders laughed too loud, had bad haircuts, others wore last year's gear, and none of us had the latest lingo. But we became best friends, and because of this it worked.

We had to take on this idea of making best friends with whomever God sent to our team. It wasn't our right to share life with our old friends, or the cool people or even people we liked! Now I'm an extrovert and have always had plenty of friends and am always collecting more, so it was a choice to treasure the few whom we were sharing this season of our lives with. This didn't mean we didn't still value and nurture some of our other friendships, particularly our long-term ones, but it did mean we learnt to find the best in whomever God sent us. It meant we changed our attitude to seeing that our team was full of gifts from God, which we were to treasure. It affected who we shared our birthdays with, socialized with, dreamt with, and prayed with.

There was no "I can't stand this person" category anymore. There was "this person is easier for me to get on with, but that more difficult person just challenges me to work harder to find out how God sees them." This was a radical shift for us. We had lots of friends and if we worked very hard we might have made it with the popular guys up front and on stage, but God showed us a new way to build a team, accepting who turned up and learning to really treasure them. And at times we were a pretty nutty bunch.

Sometimes I would wonder what the young people really thought of us. Week after week they showed up, and I figured they mainly showed up to see each other. But one day after club one of the stauncher guys was having an unusually heartfelt moment in the car park with one of the leaders. He actually said that he now believed in God because of the vibe he noticed between us as the youth leaders. Straight up! The old gospel passage of them knowing us by our love was happening for us. We were inspired by ourselves! We were learning how to live as the family of God.

When we moved from the community center into the girls' home, we were better at making our team our friends. Often at night the leaders would meet and pray in our room after the girls were supposedly settled. Inevitably it would end in chatting, laughing, eating chocolate, and, on a bad day, unloading, even crying together. We got close to those we shared our dream with, and they became our best friends. I know the girls watched these times of our sharing life together. We were closer to our leaders (and our girls) than we were to our own siblings (who we dearly love), yet we weren't blood relatives. We were a spiritual family. I think it was the best thing we offered our girls, this family-like belonging. Even now, as adults, some of our old girls and our old leaders are our close friends. And in times of crisis in our lives, they are the ones who turn up every time.

When visiting with Servants in Cambodia, I watched the team who has shared their lives together for the last decade and listened to the stories of their life together. As the season moves on and most have left Cambodia, there is the deep grief of good friendship facing separation. This same friendship is evident between them and their Cambodian friends, whom they have served and been served by in their years together. They love each other, respect each other, and have seen each other and the kingdom grow. I watch this intimacy cross over cultural and financial divides. It is a miracle. This was a God set up. They didn't take these friendships with them from New Zealand. They arrived and received these new relationships, taking them right into the center of their lives. Now the new team has come from different countries to continue the work of Servants in the urban slums. They didn't know each other but are now sharing dreams, meals, work, family, life. I watch as the cycle begins again.

It's easier in the context of overseas mission. You arrive and meet the team you will now share life with among your new neighborhood of relationships. There is no choice. If you can't make it work, you come home. Sadly, the largest reason for missionaries returning is unmanageable conflict in the team. But let's remember how many people do stay and serve fruitfully, many faithful people over many years. They have learnt how to make best friends with those God sends them. Imagine if we had this same attitude in our struggling neighborhoods at home. Rather than using all our energy crossing the city to maintain our complex web of friendship, we could focus where we are invited to be. We could take on the people God sends us.

Time after time, too many relationships is an issue for the young adults we connect with. The new age of technology makes it so much harder. Just the other day I was alongside a young woman weeping in my lounge because she wanted more time to spend on email, catching up with her many friends from all around the world. It felt like a pull away from her involvement here, but she loves being on-line, on Facebook, on Skype. There are so many good people for her to spend time with. How can she choose who to be with? I reassured her that in the end she couldn't keep up closely with a large group. It is a freedom to let go of this idea. Jesus himself had the twelve, and within this the three. He had emotional space to embrace others as they came because he wasn't trying to travel the whole time with everyone he'd ever met. He wasn't needing to spend hours each night on Facebook. Jacky Pullinger in Hong Kong says that nowadays when new missionaries arrive to their work at St. Stephens, there is a real challenge of properly connecting. "They don't leave home behind anymore!" Technology allows a person to be very connected, which isn't actually helpful for our availability to those we are suppose to be with, those who are in our here as well as our now. I have heard Servants say exactly the same of their community. The old days were simpler and in fact had a freedom about being fully present with the person in front of you. We make a big choice against the cultural tide once again here.

To do this kind of relating we need the skill of embracing the stranger and to take the risk this requires. We offer our vulnerability and leave ourselves exposed. Rejection is a real experience of community. We ask for the vulnerability of the other and sometimes take it for granted. And the damage we do to each other from our brokenness, weakness, and sinfulness is painful. It's a costly business, this kind of relationship. We can only sustain it if we have a base of acceptance in God that is solid.

For us the pain of saying goodbye is also hard and does not lessen over the years. Our children, too, have had to learn to say goodbye to people they dearly love. At times, people leave with such a sense of blessing and peace as they move on to what God is inviting them to next. But we still miss them dearly.

At other times, people leave with a sense of pain. There is sometimes a sense of anxiety or disappointment between us when expectations have not been met or hopes not realized. For us it is difficult to watch friends move away from a life of faith or back to a life of addiction. Some have left due to our failings and weaknesses. We have to choose to hold people lightly on one hand while still embracing them deeply. We have to keep our security in God so we can keep saying goodbye and choosing again. Sometimes people leave in the middle of unresolved conflict. We can learn how to use our conflict to pull us together rather than force us apart.

The birth of our first two children was a long way from the beautiful herbal home births I had dreamed of. There were complications and interventions, days of anxiety before we were free to be the new little family I had imagined. So when we had our third I was so hopeful of a chance to have a "drama free birth." But alas there were more complications and the usual incubator with us fighting with the professionals to stay by our new baby's side. It was just before Christmas, and we were coming to the end of a hard year in a tight space. Into this came a team conflict over who was to move into the new house over the road. Communication had not been clear enough, and different ones of us had thought the nicer new spot to be ours. But the team decided to sort it out late at night, just before Christmas, while I was in the hospital with a sick baby and a shattered dream of maternal bliss. We couldn't believe it. The conflict was facilitated badly, with tempers flying, tears shed, accusations made. I arrived home the next day to a chaotic house and a fractured team. I felt so hurt and betrayed. Surely this was the moment I needed them to think of me—to wash some dishes, take out the rubbish, dress the children. I was fragile, and now my husband was in a tearful mess at the end of my bed. I was over community! We were supposed to share Christmas with the team, but I had no good will to give. Even now my youngest daughter's birthday brings echoes of pain and frustration over those few days.

But Justin picked himself up, and we carried on. We realized that no one had meant it to be so bad. It was only thoughtless, not vicious. We chose to make Christmas a time of peace and joy. We chose to get over our disappointment and to forgive. The rest of our team chose to as well. And so we carried on into the New Year building bridges of trust back again as we went.

We have come to see that conflict is inevitable in community. Scott Peck talks about the journey from pseudo-community to authentic community. The difference is our response to the chaos. After the honeymoon stage inevitably there is chaos and conflict. We have a choice at this point to move back into pseudo-community or to move forward into authentic community. To move forward we go through the chaos. We see this played out time after time. People either push through the conflict and stay, having reached a deeper level with us, or they back off and move to the edge where they avoid such vulnerability.

Learning to do conflict well is therefore mandatory to healthy community. We need skills to do conflict well so it is safe and healthy and brings transformation. We need work within our lives to be peace makers, strong and resilient, able to handle conflict without it destroying us or us destroying others. It's our commitment to non violence at a personal level, and we need a theology that welcomes conflict as opportunity for this transformation. I find it reassuring to notice how the disciples struggled to go deep in their relationships without all sorts of conflict. And Jesus was with them in person!

Allowing others to belong with us and offer who they are allows God's kingdom to come a little more. We get to know others, looking for their strengths, their gifts and helping them mature. It's not easy to allow others to participate sometimes. What if they have different ideas? What if they are not as good as us in what they do? Worse still, what if they are better?

Learning to empower others in our teams and neighborhoods is the guts of the matter. It's not what we do as we are leaving or if we are sick of doing something, it's a way of functioning. At Ngatiawa we try not to do the things that others can do. Sometimes there are things we love doing and so we share those tasks. But as people learn to do things: garden, cook for a crowd, pray for someone in need, we need to step back and allow them space to have a go. I'm known to be always on about the next step. (Overseas friends mock my kiwi accent here "Neeext steep for me Jeeenny," they say.) But I am always looking for ways to help others mature and grow and I'm glad to be known for it. Sometimes it's in the inner journey, with an issue to face or a wound to find healing. Other times its in the outer activity of leading a prayer or looking after a visitor. We lead each other forward, expecting change and growth. We don't need to all be good at everything but we notice in each other what God has placed and find ways to draw it out to bless others.

We have a good friend who struggles with a mental illness. She loves to come over for dinner as long as the room is not too hot and she can choose someone she trusts to drive her home. But when she comes, she is restless, sitting around watching us prepare dinner for the guests on our community night meal. She loves housework, and when I visit her home I notice how spotless she keeps things. So we invited her to help us get the place sorted, to clean and prepare for the visitors. She is much happier this way. She comes to give to us all and we need her help, believe me!

There are times when I have shared life with people who are easier and times when it's harder, people who are talented and people who are struggling to function. Just as we don't choose our children, we can accept who God gives us and make the family of God a welcoming place. Taking on the people God sends us as our best friends is an offering that ripples out into our neighborhoods.

DON'T MISS THE POINT:

- We choose to make best friends of the people we live the dream with.

- Going deep requires letting go of some other friendships.

- We get good at saying both welcome and goodbye when we need to.

- Conflict is inevitable to authentic community.

- Conflict has the potential for healthy transformation, growth and intimacy.

- Empowering others is the heart of our call.

Look Into It

James 2:1–9 and John 13:34–35
Ask yourself: Who does the scripture tell us to include? Do I struggle to include certain types of people? Will our neighbors tell we are disciples by the way we love each other? What does this mean to us in the way we do conflict, share roles etc?

TEN

The Rhythmic Life:
Taking on Discipline and Balance

When we lived in the inner city we had a huge old house we called The Castle. In fact, it was an ugly, old mattress factory with peeling mustard-colored paint covered with graffiti. After rain, the front entrance was blocked by a rubbish-strewn lake, so we'd have to lay down a plank for guests to cross inside. It leaked badly in most rooms. Water ran down the concrete walls and sometimes into the electrics, which gave colorful displays of sparks from time to time. It had an old fireplace which heated a square meter in front of it, but the rest of the space was draughty and freezing in winter and boiling and sticky in summer. But compared to the dark, tiny office space we had squashed into during the early years, it really was a castle, full of space and light.

The door downstairs was always open, a steady flow of random, colorful visitors filing through at all hours, day and night. Sex workers and street guys called between clients for a cuppa. Team mates in the midst of life dramas showed up in tears or brimming with excitement. We were up early with little ones, ready to go another day. Our children were in preschool and playgroups, riding bikes and throwing sand round the roof, entertaining the visitors and tugging at my legs for the attention they needed. I loved all the shapes within each day, but ordering the day with all those shapes demanded energy and time. I was often sick and always tired.

At that time a young nun came to visit from a convent in Christ-church. At the time she was the youngest nun in Australasia, almost celebrity status to us. During her stay, she wore funky clothes and was not noticed as any different from the myriad of hot and alternative young adults on the street outside. Before leaving, she put on her habit (just like in *The Sound of Music*) and said something that changed our lives: "You have a great community here and I've enjoyed staying, but you will never survive this life unless you find a deeper rhythm of spirituality."

"What?" I cried internally, "did you not see our Tuesday night prayer meeting? I put a lot of time into that, preparing and pulling it off. God turned up!" But what I said was, "Thanks very much. I'll think about that."

What she said ground around inside me, and as we thought about it, we realized that she was right, of course.

For many of us, words such as "discipline" cause an allergic reaction. We imagine our rights, creativity, and fun suddenly disappearing. We see rule books, instructions, colorless rigidity. But in our community we have come to learn that the call to Jesus is a call to a life of freedom, and this freedom comes from the rhythmic life.

Since then we've had to read up and make friends with those who know how to pray, how to stop, how to listen, how to reflect. We have learned not only to love prayer but to wonder how we ever survived without our daily prayer times to think, unload, give thanks, grieve, repent, empty ourselves, listen, and plan. Though the Spirit is moving already, our coming to stillness allows us to discern where Jesus may be inviting us.

Our friend Dave Andrews (Waiters Union) taught us about how to live an "intercession led life," where we learn (in Dave's words) to "respond not react." As our involvement deepens with people in messy places, the needs are so overwhelming. As our lives become complicated with friend-ships, marriage, and then later kids, the demands on us are huge.

I used to seek God annually as I discerned the direction of the year ahead. Now I seek him daily as I discern the day ahead. In fact I've learnt to hold a frame of being, where often throughout the day I am in prayer as I decide all the many small choices. I have learnt to rush less, to blast less, and to allow the Spirit to lead me. And if I can do it, anyone can. I am the great bulldozer, the activist (or the activity-ist, which might not mean quite the same thing), the dreamer, schemer, squeeze-the-most-out-of-the-orange kind of person. And despite my initial apprehension, this has been good news for me. Surely this is the bonus of a living relationship with a God who wants to be my friend and guide, who knows more about me and what's happening than I do.

Spending time with our friends in the Community of the Transfiguration in Melbourne (a place of daily communal prayer, with monks who are the real deal, with robes and beards and cool kinds of chants) helped us reflect on our rhythm of life back home. So now at Ngatiawa, we gather each morning, noon, and evening, "bookending" our day and night in prayer. As tired Pentecostals, we have also reclaimed the joy of liturgy. Liturgy holds us up on a long and tiring day. We don't always have to make it all happen in a service; we don't have to put lots of energy into creating something new. Sometimes we still like to plan and prepare around a theme—our friend calls it "soak." But sometimes we gather and join something planned for us already in the prayer book, full of truth and beauty and Scripture. It's reassuring for to pray these older prayers that we share with others around the country and world, because it keeps us mindful of the wider story we belong to. It reminds us of our humanness, that we're just a speck on the timeline.

It cracks me up that we keep running out of our prayer books and have to rely on an ally on our parish staff to slip us more. Ironically while the church is feeling tired of the prayer book and looking for something less formal, we're slipping them out the back door by the boxful, like a drug deal. I guess rebellion takes many forms. We prepare the table with a candle and some stones, maybe a cross or a piece of sculpture, and the liturgy helps hold sacred moments in a sustainable way.

We also learned from our friends in UNOH Melbourne about the importance of keeping the Sabbath, a day each week where we set aside a good chunk of time for God—to sleep, pray, think, read, write. It's far easier to keep going through a busy week when a Sabbath day is coming to recharge us for the week ahead. We have learned from many sources, but my current favorite is Abraham Heshel's book on *The Sabbath*. He thinks that what the Jewish community offers the world more than anything else (not counting God himself, of course) is the sacred place of the Sabbath.

Having gotten better at keeping Sabbath, it now seems so vile to me, the endlessness of our consumer lifestyle, where every day is busy, rushing and shopping. I look forward to my Sabbath and always know how many sleeps away it is.

Added to this are our rhythms of team retreating, community-wide times of gathering and drawing aside, and times of personal retreat too. We also take holidays away from our busy households, sometimes as families and couples, sometimes as friends.

The gift of our land has helped us with these rhythms. We're creating a sacred space we hope reflects the heart of our contemplative life as a movement. We have prayer huts and a chapel and beautiful riverside spaces to find our strength again.

Our city teams, too, have grown over the years in their commitment to this prayerful life and meet daily and weekly to pray together and alone. They, too, have made sacred spaces in their own lives and homes and gardens. Our team in the Newtown Park flats has a prayer room right in the middle of the high density flats. Others have a special corner of a room, a place to draw aside to. But it's not just the physical spaces, although they help; it's the internal space and attitude which has deepened in us over the years.

You would think it would make us far less efficient on the ground, with an increase of time in prayer and contemplation, but the reality for us has been the opposite. I am sure that I am now far more fruitful in the kingdom than I used to be. I am better able to function in the team and better able to go for it without getting sick. I know when to respond to a need and when to leave it. I still get distracted, driven, and anxious (although I did give up anxiety for Lent this year), but I can feel a complete change to our approach these days, and it is part of our growing humility to allow God's spirit space in our lives.

In observing many other communities around the world over the last decade, we have been encouraged on this path. We find that all those we know who began like us as high-energy activist types have either found a contemplative center or collapsed. We also have found movements that began as contemplative prayerful groups and have added action and hospitality, justice and reconciliation to their lives. It seems to work both ways.

Other things, too, are part of the rhythm: sleeping well, exercising, working in life-giving jobs, eating well, working together in some shared tasks, even sharing our finances.

Both individually and as a community we have to find the balance between enough room for spontaneity, creativity, and new movement, with enough shape and structure to hold us together and keep us solid. Our friends in Inner Change speak of "soft walls."

Within our teams, there is also a difference in what is healthy at different ages and stages of life. We came to realize as we grew older that what had been a healthy rhythm when we were younger needed to change. What bought life, what sustained life each season, was very different.

That long-ago night when Justin asked our mentor Charles Ringma for his wisdom for twenty-year-olds, he also asked him for wisdom for thirty- and forty-year-olds. While he challenged the twenty-year-olds to high energy and action, thirty-year-olds must develop a stronger contemplative life to uphold their activism, and forty-year-olds must start to mentor others. No longer do they only push their dreams, but they help the dreams of others become reality.

So for our younger adults, setting some rhythms helps keep their Jesus center alive, but we don't expect many of them to be asking for longer times of prayer and silence. We, the older ones, need to keep challenging our comfort levels and stay actively engaged with the margins. Married life and then babies come, and we fill up life, nestle down. But what about the call to the poor? What about our commitment to serving together? The action becomes harder, but it is okay to love our retreat time and to need more of it to function well.

Personality plays a part here too. For some of us we find a rhythm which helps us to do enough of the important things each day. It helps us block out the distractions, avoid the things that destroy us and others and our passion for the kingdom. For others, though, the rhythm helps us not do too much. It stops the passionate or the "super caring" from burning out, from losing themselves into the abyss of others' needs, from becoming overwhelmed or resentful.

For all of us, a good rhythm allows us to live more easily in the face of the consumer machine. In the same way that alcoholics in recovery have no option but to live a disciplined life for the rest of their lives, I am a self-seeking consumer addicted to luxury, in recovery for the rest of my life. I realized how our addictions worked as I shared my life with other addicts. We too, in hard times, reach back for the things which will ease our pain, numb our conviction, remove difficult challenges. I want to buy something: chocolate, coffee, a cool new frock, a movie, a night in a hotel. I need to buy something. Learning to say no to my incessant need for more will always be hard for me. My life rhythm helps me live true to my convictions that this is not the answer. At the end of a disciplined day I can find some joy knowing that I have not destroyed the planet, others, or myself. In fact I'm adding to the good news round the place. And God feels closer when I take away all the barriers I place between us.

The main point remains that living a disciplined life helps me not to confuse myself with God. I have to admit I do get confused. I have mistaken myself for God many times. Super missionary to the people in pain! I can change everything! But then the overwhelming reality of the state of the planet, the lives of my crazy mixed-up friends, and of course my own chaos as I look in the mirror, lead me to paralysis. Help! This is too hard! I can't change anything!

When I accept that God is in fact the one who has the answers, the truth, the plan, and I merely have to follow him, I can continue to get up in the morning. I can to learn to "yoke up" and let him carry the load that my compassion burdens me with (as well as my brokenness, which burdens me even more). I can know that I only have to respond today to the invitation of today. I can accept my own invitations and leave others to respond to theirs. I can trust that as God calls me, he will also provide me with what I need.

A disciplined life reminds us that we need to pray, we need to rest, we need to respond to poverty and justice, we need to play, we need God, and we need his people.

Don't Miss the Point

- A healthy rhythm of discipline saves our lives, others' lives, and the planet!

- We stay close to Jesus through discipline; it brings freedom to us.

LOOK INTO IT

Matt 14:13–36 and 2 Peter 1:5–7
Ask yourself: Do I have a good balance of life? Do I have a rhythm that helps me stay faithful to my sense of calling?

ELEVEN

The Simple Life:
Taking on Justice, Grace, and Generosity

In the early days Justin and I met some inspiring types in the Catholic Worker world in Brisbane. As we began to recognize the destructive cycles of consumerism on our planet, a friend of ours asked, "If you were to help a group of young adults like these guys know how to start consuming in a better way, what would your advice be?" With a deadpan face, the Catholic Worker guy said, "Don't consume." An awkward silence followed. "Yes sure, but if you were going to help us find a place to start . . . ?" Again, a pause. "No, just don't consume!" It did our heads in.

So because we were disturbed, we were passionate to start living the alternative somehow. So we started along, eating less meat, shopping at op shops, using recycled shopping bags. Like all the justice issues, we needed to start somewhere, and we enjoyed the challenge.

As we talked about justice and simplicity, in seeped our pride and competitiveness (who could eat more chick peas in a week), along with our judgment. Life began to lose joy as we sacrificed everything for the sake of simplicity. We laughed when we were accused by a friend (who was embarrassed of us) at a social event of "dressing down for the poor!" But what did we actually mean by "for the poor?" Was all our talk and justice giving anything to others? Our antidote came in finding the missing piece of the puzzle: generosity.

We changed our language from a "simple lifestyle" to a "generous lifestyle." We went with less *in order that* others could have more. It was a significant shift. We didn't want to be known for what we went with-out or what we weren't allowed. We didn't want a culture where everyone focused on what they were doing without. That felt like a stingy life. We wanted to be known for our generosity, for what we gave away, for where we helped. We wanted to be generous with all our lives.

Spending less money allows us to have more money to give away. It allows us to share what we have materially with others. We are learning to look after what we have, to reuse and recycle. We are learning to be more responsible with the planet, taking less of the resources and adding less to the rubbish pile. In fact we have learnt that we can survive with so much less than we thought. Even the simple discipline of really thinking before we buy anything has slowed the cash flow significantly. I try to have a gap between when I think I need something and when I buy it, in case during the gap, I think up an alternative. Sometimes I can borrow something from someone or can actually do without it. Sometimes the "need" fades quite fast.

Sharing life together has helped us here. The joy and necessity of com-munity is that between us, we use less. We swap clothes, furniture, cars, blackware (TVs, DVD players, etc.), garden tools appliances, tools, baby stuff . . . . And if we need something else we ask round at our churches. I'd like to say we share everything "except toothbrushes," but there was once a time . . . . Living at the girls' home I noticed one day that there was one less toothbrush than those of us living in the house. There were around ten of us, so it was hard to keep track sometimes. In putting it out there that someone seemed to have hidden their toothbrush, one young woman shamelessly stated, "I don't have one, I've never had one." Everyone went quiet. My heart sank. She had been living with us for six months. She was not known for her health or hygiene practices. "How do you brush your teeth?" I asked quietly. "I just grab one, any one and use it." She shot us a gleaming, toothy smile.

But the danger of getting good at recycling is hoarding, which is par-ticularly rife among those drawn to the crazy life of community in general (not a fifty-fifty balance of orderly types). Also those who have had less early on or who have had other things lacking in their own family life tend to make up for it later by never throwing anything away. We had a young woman who used to hide stuff under her bed—clothing, games, leftover food . . . . It did take me a few months to track down the smell in her room.

You can imagine the tensions when the "hoarders" share life with the "chuckers." The "chuckers" can include those who can confuse personal peace of mind with clean and tidy external spaces or those who have a power issue and find an arena to take some control. But in favor of the chuckers (okay, I myself am among these guys), simplicity is not just about cheaper or not spending, it's about less.

When we went travelling, we did a huge throw out so as to allow space for others to live in our home (paying our bills and running our community, God bless them). Boxes of our life went off to the op shop, some into storage. We then lived out of one case each for six months. It wasn't hard, it was great! I realized again the freedom of less: less choice, less cleaning, less hassle. In getting back I couldn't really think of what I had stored that I actually needed or missed, other than photo albums and some books. So we did another big throw. We had learnt while we were away that we could survive well in smaller spaces too. So we found we could fit in half our house on our return, and another couple was able to move in with us.

It frustrates me when I watch people become passionate about the Jesus lifestyle but who can't actually relocate to get involved because they have too much stuff. This has actually happened around us many times.

We had a young woman doing well in her early discipleship. She had faced some major challenges in her life and things were still tough. Her mum loved her dearly, so when she announced she was considering moving back in with us as part of our community, her Mum went out and bought her a king-sized bed. She then had to continue the payments on it herself, until it was paid off. Living in the inner city, this was problematic since space was tight; we had to share rooms to afford rent. Suddenly the whole discussion around whether she should she move in and where God was calling her to became centered on what could work best for her bed! Bravely she moved in, bed and all. More bravely still was the woman who offered to share a room with her. There was literally a few spare centimeters of floor space in that room, which allowed for the bucket to catch the leaks.

There is a time to nest in life, to know where we come from, where we belong, to establish a good sense of healthy home. Sometimes we have had to move round as young adults too often in our community due to rent increases or tenancy agreements, etc. But what a gift it is when someone is free to move in response to the needs of those on the margins. How wonderful it is when someone can swap houses to take on a certain role or serve the community needs. Travelling light is a gift to others and a freedom to ourselves.

Again, our friend St. Francis teaches us that when we own nothing, all God's creation belongs to us. It's true, I've noticed when I have less stuff in my life, simple things become a huge pleasure. When travelling I was so aware of the spaces around me, particularly the landscape. I had little concern for my things, my clothes, my furniture. Time in creation, a good meal with a friend, a sing around the fire outside—these were the good things of the day. The good things in life are not those in the adverts. I think I really believe that!

I notice with my friends who have their lives stripped back the most that when something special is made or created, how much they appreciate it. They have an eye for beauty that is so discerning. They have taught me to buy less and to treasure more by the process of making it and creating it, a far richer experience. I guess the whole slow food movement can transfer to many things. Slow food honors a slow and intensive process towards good food: home grown, homemade, loving labor of a known and dignified source. Surely the same is valued in sewing clothes, crafting gifts, making or restoring furniture.

Principles of permaculture have also been inspiring us in these issues. Our friend Jarrod from Peace Tree community in Perth talks about it as "good news to the land." I think there is "good news to the worker" and "good news to the land." We try to head for these things, cut out the middle-man.

Now when I have an experience of consuming something all packaged up but lacking beauty and loving crafting I feel quite sick inside. I realize I've come a way down the track. The fact that a while ago I wouldn't notice at all makes me question what else in my life is choked up, still unrecognized and destructive. It's like when you spend time outside the West in a place where women's bodies are covered up in respect and then you arrive back to the West and our shameless nudity and sexually driven appetite seems suddenly so hideous. You wonder why you didn't see it before.

But a simple life is also about time. Needing less means needing to work for money less. This allows more time for the people who need us. We have thought a lot around the professionalism of good development and community work. There is always a limit to professional approaches to people and poverty, needs which cannot be met by professionals. Working with young women in care for years we rubbed up with lots of amazing professionals: social workers, counselors, lawyers. And we also rubbed up with some terrible ones. There are those people in the job for the wrong motives, those badly matched in their roles, those fiscally driven to make things work financially. Even the good ones are so constrained by their budgets and time frames that I truly believe they cannot do their jobs well and I feel sorry for them. They work under enormous pressure.

We live with a social worker who on starting his work was struggling to attend to all his "clients" in the working week. One day at his desk he came across another file with a long list of names with his name allocated to them. When he asked, his supervisor told him not to worry about that list, to just stick to the ones he already had. He didn't last long in the job, but he does continue to share his life with those who are struggling. He has a few people now to whom he is committed as a good friend rather than an unending list of people he cannot even get to meet.

One of the girls in our care had been living with us for a long time. On experiencing some further trauma, she became unsafely depressed and had to be put into temporary hospital care. Suddenly a new supervisor became involved with the case who from the start didn't like us. Possibly there were insecurity issues or a prejudice against Christians, but suddenly she had all the power and we had none. The young woman was scared and angry and wanted to come home to us. I reassured her that we were not giving up on her, but then the system relocated her from one institution to another. In her anger she protested, and within a fortnight she was locked down for six months in a junior jail, having had a good physical hiding from the staff there. The system had turned a sad girl into a bad girl before my eyes, the consequences played out for months ahead. Luckily she remains a close friend of ours. In the end, the system couldn't reach her the way we could. We had the hours to spend, we had no budgets to meet, and we didn't have too many others to squeeze in. What she needed was love, care, friendship, long-term belonging, and discipleship. Professionalism cannot offer this, but neither can we if our lives are not simple enough to make space.

But we can eat only rice, spend our lives with the poor, and yet still remain crowded and chaotic souls. Simplicity at this deeper, internal level is our greatest challenge.

At best, I am a high-energy and creative person. But due to my own wounds, I am also competitive and ambitious and full of fear of failure. I struggle with needing to please everyone, to be perceived as onto it, to be in control. My love of life can cross the line for a greed for life. Doing everything, pleasing everyone, and being the best at it all is truly exhausting! Thankfully, I live among truth tellers and my own journey with Jesus has been full of grace, enough to help me offload. My friends have encouraged me to slow down, do less, stop competing with the unseen audience. It's not unusual for conversations among us to include gentle joking about the things I struggle with. "Oh, oh here comes the bulldozer," someone said the other day. "Sometimes you need the bulldozer," I was quick to respond. It feels good to be on a level where we are well known for better and worse and loved anyway.

In fact the liberation for me has come in understanding that God calls me not only to have less but to do less. We don't have to save the whole world. His call does not drive us to the ground. He helps us live the moment and appreciate what and who we have right in front of us. We have begun to stop needing more. Our internal space has simplified.

So we make progress on a simple lifestyle in order to live a generous lifestyle—and the outward journey is prophetic to others and frees us up. Too often we hear, "they burnt out," around mission and community, but our perspective is that most people "busy out" in their overcrowded lives. For those who do risk burn out, the call to simple inner life is their salvation.

DON'T MISS THE POINT

- Generous lifestyle is a wonderful and just way to live.

- To reach this freedom we embrace simplicity.

- Less is better for everyone.

- Simplicity includes our time, our space and our stuff.

- Simplicity also includes our soul, our inner life.

Look Into It

Luke 9:1–6

Ask yourself: What unnecessary things are you taking on the journey? What stops you from taking on a generous lifestyle?

TWELVE

The Transformed Life:
Taking on Hope for Change

An artist who lived among the street community in the rough end of our city came each week for church at the Castle. With fiery dark eyes, deep wrinkles all over his face, and a pudding bowl of thick black hair, he was as colorful as the art he painted. Each week during the service, he would open a large bottle of Coke with a long, loud hiss, standing up in the middle of prayers to lift his hands in the air, staring out at something, possibly sizing up an angle for a painting. If anyone crossed him, his explosive tongue would lash out with obscenities and abuse, his walking cane waving madly in the air.

His eyesight was deteriorating and this worried him, but drawn by God's kindness, he cried out for healing, and when God answered his prayer, he began to be transformed. One evening someone stepped across him in the crowded room, accidentally knocking his cane and spilling his Coke. As expected, he fiercely shouted, "f*** off!" But then his face melted into a large smile, he put his head to the side and gently added, "please."

Jesus didn't come simply to save us for heaven, but to change us along the way. Those who hung round Jesus went from being timid, bickering, confused, and small-minded to leading the biggest movement in history, full of power and boldness. They went from living the quiet life of earning a crust and looking after themselves to sharing what they had with a growing church and those who had need in their neighborhood. Everything in their outer lives changed and internally this transformation changed them. Or look at Paul, not Christ in perfection for sure, but what change compared to his earlier years. He was transformed from an aggressive, powerful, abusive type to a strong servant leader. In following Jesus, we don't lose ourselves, but find our best selves.

In challenging Mum during a silly conflict we'd had, Dad simply said, "Don't get uptight she'll never change these things and neither will you. You have always been like that. And your Mum has always been like this since I have known her all those years ago." I was fuming. I wanted some things in Mum to change. I wanted some things in me to change too. Which things were things we were born with? Which things were about our choices, and which things were about something else, something unhealthy that had developed in us? I spent the next few years working this out.

In terms of the destructive personal baggage we carry, it can be divided into three categories: our sin, our weakness, and our brokenness.

Our sin is a result of selfish, destructive choices we make that damage ourselves and others. Our response to sin is to repent, to turn round and make better choices. I had an issue with fear in my life, but I chose to watch horror movies as a teenager that disturbed me deeply and added terror to my life. I needed to stop doing that. It was not healthy. I have had seasons of life where I cope with my anxiety by eating chocolate and when I'm not eating chocolate, I'm wishing I were, and that makes me grumpy. It was an unhealthy choice and I needed to stop.

The opposite to sin is fruit and maturity, which both arise out of the constructive choices we make, choices that bring life to others and build up others and ourselves. Because I have chosen against my greed, others can share my home and my life. Because I have learned to pray instead of eat chocolate, I am maturing in my faith.

There are some things in our lives that trip us up and seem to come without our choice. It feels like we always struggle with these issues, always pull against them. I have an issue with overpowering people. My great ideas and my energy in the task can feel bossy, domineering, and disempowering to others. This is not sin. I didn't choose to be like this. It is the weakness of my strength, the shadow side if you like. I have reclaimed the term "bulldozer," handed to me at times by those around me. Now that I live in the country, I realize that a bulldozer can cut a track where there is none, go in first and mark the way. I pioneer new paths and see things that don't yet exist, bringing them into being. I will always be a bulldozer, because I am created to be one. Bulldozers have weaknesses, and it is my responsibility to always be aware of how I manage that. But I can't avoid it.

As we become more self-aware, we can also develop and mature a healthy sense of our strengths and gifts. How liberating to know you are not competing with others, nor do you have to be strong in everything. A community full of healthy people offering their strengths and gifts to each other, an image of the body functioning.

Lastly, our brokenness causes destruction. None of us gets through this messy and painful world untouched. We are all damaged along the way. This wounds us emotionally and, at best, we are left scarred.

I grew up as a "good girl" in my family. In some ways I was easy to parent, and so the expectation on me was to please and perform well, which I did. But it wounded me with an aversion to conflict, a fear of failure, a fear of letting others down. I struggle with pressure to over function to please and impress. Partly I need to make good choices as I deal with this, to put in boundaries, to stop doing too much. Partly my strengths of being high energy and high capacity will always leave me with a liability for over-performing. I needed to be aware of this in myself, but I also needed to find some healing.

As we face the feelings we so desperately work to avoid, we uncover the source of our wound. And as we face up to the deceptions in our lives and replace them with the truth, we discover the opposite of our wounding, which is our healing. What a huge part of the good news this is! How lightly we say the truth will set us free, but it does! I have had many privileged sessions of prayer and reflection with people as they face up to their painful places and find new truth that changes their lives.

All areas of our baggage require courage and honesty to look in the mirror. We can create a culture within our community life that not only requires each other to look in the mirror but makes it as easy as possible to allow this transformation to happen. It's a gift we offer to our neighbors as well.

First we must create a space of belonging. We make space for others to come; we invite them in. When people know they are part of the family they can begin to unload. Then we have a high value around grace and acceptance, which helps us bring our guards down.

In one of those crazy musicals we pulled together, my friend was invited to join in. Loveable yet messy, he lived at the time in a clothing bin. Tall and thin, he could slide himself through the slot each night into the warmer clothing pile inside, kind of like posting himself to bed. With his addiction to glue he often was high in more ways than one, the clothing bin had no shower facility. In came a great young woman from Urban Vision, his dance partner for the show. He tells us now of his nerves at her loveliness as she bravely took his shaking hands. Unwell from the hard life, one evening he left the rehearsal to throw up outside. Embarrassed he tried to clean himself up a little. Knowing he was stinking and messy, he nervously returned to the dancing. Smiling on his return, she simply took his hands again and carried on dancing without a flinch. He said at that moment he knew he had found something among us that was different, an acceptance that allowed him to find a new way of life. He now holds down a good job and a flat. We make the spaces for others welcoming.

Then we introduce our friends to a God who loves them. It's important we do this through our words and our actions. This work of transformation is not up to us—it's God's work. We must be clear where the grace comes from, where the freedom and truth flows from, where the power for change is sourced. We find that at this point some run from the light, a sad choice, but their choice. We always say we'll work with you, but we won't work against you. We don't force anyone or pressure anyone; it's nonsense to God's invitation to do so. God's love is a magnet that draws us.

Our friends from the Mennonite community in Sydney teach us the three A's. First, create an *alternative*. This will then be *attraction*. Then be ready to *articulate*. So our role is to create the space which will draw others towards God's love. When they are ready to search, they will ask us, and we will be ready to help them understand God's invitation for them.

Establishing a culture of vulnerability and transparency is vital, but it needs to be nurtured in an atmosphere of care, acceptance, and grace. Transformation happens most easily in a context of grace. Grace is not a cultural norm down here in Wellington. We are cynical and harsh folk. For us to learn to be gracious has been a long, hard, and conscious road. When people move in, early on we begin holding up the mirror gently, in small ways, in order to establish the culture of "round here we speak into each other's lives." "How come you hate going to prayer meetings?" "How come you are angry when we talk about money?" Asking questions that allow others to search is far more empowering than passing judgment or even offering reflections. It forces someone to do their own work deeply. The right question unlocks forbidden areas, allowing light and truth to come on in. The answer is often different than what we would first assume.

Lots of this work of transformation comes through conflict in community. Through the rub and grit of sharing life, we learn a lot about ourselves. We learn what we're good at and what we're not. We learn to question our reactions and our motivations. We are challenged to look inside and to be vulnerable and transparent with each other. Over time I can truly look back and notice the changes in all of us. In fact often I find myself saying to someone new, "Yes he is annoying, but believe me, compared to what he used to be like, he has changed!" We have learnt that learning to do conflict well is one of the greatest gifts you can bring. It helps maximize this transformation and it helps to minimize further damage.

Transformation is the work of the Spirit at every level, not only personal, but communal and corporate. We work for the transformation of our society at a neighborhood level, a wider society level, a systemic level, and in the widest world of power and politics which rule over us.

Our friends lived for years in the council flats. They were disturbed when the local city council decided to put the rent up. They rallied round a group of tenants and supporters and slept outside the council buildings for a few days, bringing attention to the issue. At the council meeting, they challenged the mayor with scriptural stories of justice and caring for the poor. To save face the council agreed to go to referendum, confident that the average council rate payer would opt for the rent rise at no cost and good benefit to them. However, there was time then to get out and educate the wider community on the reality of council flats, the struggle many had with paying rent each week, the small spaces, and the security issues. In fact, many "average rate payers" could understand that when it was put to them, and the council lost support for the rent rise. Our friends were asked to leave the flats but hundreds of rent-payers were prevented from a crippling rent rise that year.

When East Timor was invaded by Indonesia in the 1990s, we had a problem with our government continuing to train their air force as they massacred innocent victims in their neighbor's land. We would vigil each Thursday night outside defense, praying and raising awareness to the public. Other activities were planned by peace groups, and we were able to join in. One of our guys burnt an Indonesian flag outside parliament as part of our protest. Eventually, he was arrested, although his action was actually not illegal. As it went through the court system, which resulted in the police being fined $10,000 (that this guy then gave to the people of East Timor), we were able to bring more pressure.

Much later when Indonesia finally left, East Timorese activist leaders visited Wellington, inviting our flag burner to a gathering where they expressed their thanks. They said many groups in Australia and New Zealand had applied pressure to governments to respond, which had been vital to ending the occupation. In hearing that, we were so encouraged that we can change the world, even the biggest, ugliest parts of the world. We have drawn so much inspiration from our mentors Martin Luther King Jr., Dorothy Day, William Wilberforce, Te Whiti Orongomai, and others who made deep and lasting changes on the world around them.

So often believers come from one end or the other, either all about personal transformation or all about social transformation. But they belong together; one gives authenticity to the other. So let's pursue transformation on every level. It's not easy, but possible, vital, and hopeful. Jesus doesn't offer us a ticket to a distant, happier, ever-after-land called heaven later. He promises lifelong change within ourselves and those we love now. So we wrestle with injustice and demand change now.

I feel so frustrated when we accommodate our brokenness, sinfulness, and weakness so we never have to look in the mirror. But this kills the work of the kingdom. Transformation is a principle we live by. We have faith to see lives changed this side of eternity.

Don't Miss the Point

- Having a theology of transformation is central to the gospel.

- Transformation is our hope for the world and for us.

- Transformation is a reality within a living relationship with God.

LOOK INTO IT

Philippians 1:6 and Luke 19:1–9
Ask yourself: How is God inviting transformation in your life? Where do you see God's transformation around you?

THIRTEEN

The Reconciled Life:
Taking on the Work of Mending

On sabbatical, our family had the privilege of staying with some Carmelite nuns in The Holy Hill Hermitage in Ireland (try it with an Irish accent). Imagine a beautiful, desolate Irish landscape complete with old castles, rugged coastlines, and summer day temperature requiring a warm jersey. Theirs was a life dedicated to prayer and solitude, and their community life centered around being "together alone." You have to say that over a few times slowly to really get it. How can we be alone and together at the same time? This was a long way from my comfortable evangelical background of noisy services with the happy and clappy din of a good Sunday. (It's not surprising Pentecostals don't do that several times a day like the Carmelites—no one could handle the pace.)

For these Irish nuns, hospitality was to offer the desert to others, and they built beautiful, simple stone hermitages over their rolling land. They met together daily to pray and shared a communal meal with their guests once a week. Their weekly rhythm worked out at three days of solitude, three days of shared work, and one day of Sabbath, "a day in eternity." Another deep idea! The Sabbath we shared included many in the local community, filling their beautiful chapel, and afterward we shared a simple meal together. Then music, singing and dancing (an Irish jig!) broke out in the courtyard, robes and all!

I loved their joy in Scripture, their desire to spend a life in prayer. I learnt of their choices toward this hermit's life, their growing desires that led them to dedicate themselves so deeply to God. I loved the symbols of their tradition, the water features in the garden (that's a Carmelite thing), the candles, and the altar.

It was a wonderful lifestyle, a gem in the kingdom. They saw their calling to pray and intercede not for themselves but for others, for the world. They didn't just aspire to a deep prayer life or talk about it, they actually did it, and you could tell from the atmosphere of the place. It was a gift to us, allowing us space to be inspired and attend to some major personal issues that had sprung up within us as we rested from ministry. I was aware of how little I knew of these traditions, this calling in the kingdom. Where had I been hiding to miss all this?

In contrast, we also visited the Steiger community in Minneapolis. Steiger is a shamelessly evangelical community based in the U.S. They are passionate about telling people about Jesus. They mix with colorful folks across their city and offer hospitality in a number of community houses attached to an informal, fringy kind of church space, The Salvage Yard. This wasn't church on the pews or in a beautiful chapel, and it certainly wasn't silence. It was couches and coffee and piercing and tattoos. It wasn't robes and stability; it was roaming types in dramatic gears.

I was able to go out on a Friday night with some of their team who meet in the roughest end of town in the shadow of a high-density block known as the "crack stack." Huddled in a small shed at the back of the buildings, they gathered at 10:00 p.m. to pray. They assured me we were allowed to use the shed for a "team meeting" and, judging by the smell in the place, no one was using it much anyway. They arrived one by one, and it felt like some sort of illegal church gathering. As I heard the neighborhood winding up outside, my adrenaline started pumping! Then right outside the anarchist, punk "Café of Hard Knocks," they set up their Jesus kitchen. No surprises about what they stand for in the neighborhood. They are the Jesus freaks, arriving faithfully week after week, late night, and often in between. They offer a free rice dish and hot coffee to those gathering late night on the streets. They talk to people, often the same people each week, who love to come for their coffee and company. They talk about Jesus, about life, about pain and hard times. I loved it! I was missing home, and it inspired me to continue sharing my life with the poor, particularly those trapped in the urban jungles of our world.

Here was another gem of the kingdom—in some ways on the other end of a continuum from our friends in robes in the Holy Hill Hermitage, yet clearly both so much part of the kingdom. In fact the evangelicals were learning to be more serious in reflection and prayer, and the Carmelites were very keen to explain all about their lifestyle and calling to their many visitors. Both communities were faithful, full of truth and hope and love. Both were full of the Jesus Spirit.

As I reflected on my experience of church in growing up, I felt sad that so often there was a huge divide between these kinds of groups and callings. I grew up in an Anglican tradition that was too slow to embrace the charismatic gifts, a Baptist youth group that had no time for social justice, a Pentecostal church that never explored the depth of silence, and a university Christian group that struggled to engage with the poor outside themselves. It seems so obvious to me that these divides are unhelpful and leave us starved of vital blood flow around the body.

In fact I now consider the biblical analogy of the body of Christ and often experience the reality as the skeleton of Christ. Each part of the church is lying still in its own spot, unconnected and therefore not living and moving properly.

As we journeyed around the world, I realized how vast the kingdom of God is: from the silence and huge gathering of reconciliation of Taize in France, to the work of Servants and Inner Change in the slums of Asia's urban poor neighborhoods. How big is our God, how creative are his people, how broad is the invitation, and how much we need each other!!

Because Urban Vision community has been interdenominational, we have been able to draw more easily from many streams. We love action with the activists, evangelism with the conservatives, liturgy with Anglicans, contemplation with the Catholics, and we love to engage with a good Pentecostal Holy Spirit time of worship (bring out the dancing shoes!). We have drawn good strength from many traditions and allowed the expressions of many gifts and callings. The challenge has been to cross the divide between the radical edges of the church and the center of the institutional church, for we can be just as much a part of a divide from our ecumenical position here on the edge. And who says what God sees as the edge and the center anyway?

It must be a sadness for God, how often one part of the kingdom is so completely separated from the other—kind of like a parent whose kids are not talking to each other. The fantastic young adults we find in one community or congregation often have no respect for others, and we have recognized this ignorance and pride in ourselves as well.

But now we think there is a place of calling and charism. The Carmelites offer something to the Steiger community. We are each called to be something unique and to offer this gift to the world. We belong to a certain part of the body and align with certain traditions, which is healthy and necessary. But it is also necessary to acknowledge the vastness of the kingdom and to humbly admit our smallness in the great story of God's people. We can't be all things to all people—what a relief! As we humbly draw from others, we learn and appreciate the differences they bring.

We have also come to recognize the difference between judgment and critique, between competition and rubbing shoulders to produce maturity. We need to encourage the latter and reject the former, and finding that line isn't easy, particularly among young radicals with a lot of "against" kind of energy. As we search for truth, we need to listen to others' perspectives and respond reflectively instead of defensively or aggressively.

A preacher in our town recently spoke out against social justice in favor of evangelism, an unhelpful frame for the young adults listening. His point that social justice can allow us to neglect the valuable gift of evangelism is true and helpful but to replace one for another is neither scriptural nor unifying. How much better if we change our "or" statements to "and" ones.

We have a concept in Urban Vision of "digging for the gold." We look for what is true and beautiful, challenging and kingdom bringing, wherever we connect. We now choose consciously to connect across the body in what we read, what we attend, and who we connect with. Finding and building on the commonality is always helpful. So many others have fed into the life and health of our community as we dig for the treasure. We often find we disagree with others, see things differently, prioritize differently, respond differently, but in light of full truth, all of us will have some things wrong, and I suspect God is not so worried over some of the things we may feel are the big issues of difference.

We have friends who are part of the Catholic Worker community here in New Zealand (Hokianga, Christchurch, and Otaki), a tradition of peace making and activism steeped in prayer, community, and hospitality to the poor. Recently they were involved in an action to bring attention and protest to the U.S. spy base in our country, which our government funds in secret each year to the tune of multi-million dollars. Many Christians I know would struggle to understand their view and priority, write them off as extremists. But they challenge and inspire us as they help us think of the world from the perspective of the families in Iraq who have been bombed and broken, of those who could be fed in the world with the money we spend each hour on munitions. Suddenly, their actions make more sense to me, and I am grateful for their passion and courage to raise these difficult issues. Their challenge that our society is not fair and just is uncomfortable, but it is a valuable perspective of the kingdom.

Of course there are things we hold to be non-negotiable, serious convictions from God, and we need to know where our bottom lines are. In Urban Vision, we belong deeply to the body and our involvement in the hurting world. We cannot back down from our Jesus Center—what it means for us to follow Jesus. That doesn't mean we can't work with others on a different page, and it doesn't mean that everyone must agree with us or change to be like us, but it's what we agree on within Urban Vision.

But we suspect that as Christians we can have far fewer bottom lines than we think, and that we can actually disagree on lots of things. We have come to learn that there is far more that we can live with peacefully, agreeing to disagree. We value consensus, but sometimes consent is a lot easier to give and receive. This is an idea from the Waiter's Union that we have found helpful.

In biblical times, the early church had conflict over the eating of food offered to idols. This was much larger for them than the tensions between justice and evangelism or action and contemplation. But did they split the church over it? No, the wisdom was that each could eat according to their own conscience and not judge the others. Unity was more important to them. Unity is one of the most radical signs of the kingdom of God.

Here in New Zealand there are cultural divides between Māori and Pākehā. Our commitment to bi-culturalism has been one of the most challenging, painful, and rewarding parts of our journey. The evils of colonialism don't make an easy backdrop for us to begin with, but our road is connected to reconciliation, justice, peace, and well-being for our land and its people. There has not been one right way to cross the divide, but there have certainly been lots of wrong ways.

Early on as a teacher's college student, I felt increasingly convicted of the place of Māori within our education system. Māori students were not doing as well as Pākehā, and I was full of guilt from the history of my colonial ancestors, nervous as I began to walk what felt like a landmine of anger and pain. During this time, we had a club of young people, and it was obvious that our Māori kids struggled with issues of identity, education, health, and home life. We wanted to help them find their potential, their dreams and their place in God's family as Māori.

So we launched out in ignorant bliss and booked the teacher's college *marae* (meeting house). I knew well the high value on *powhiri* (welcome ceremony) and *tikanga* (culture/ways of doing things) in the college *marae*. I had my classes there, and there was a staunch sense of pride about the place. So you can imagine my horror when a few hours prior to our arrival, our speaker bailed in favor of a better social offer at the rugby club. Frantically we "dialed a *powhiri*" but no one seemed available. We had an American friend who had learnt a speech in Māori from a conservative Christian ("heaven is my *marae*, the blood of Christ is my river. . . "), but it wasn't the right feel for the teacher's college *marae*. Poor Justin, there are those moments when it is so good not to be a bloke (and who said gender equity was that important anyway, bring on the old traditions I thought). He stood up in front of my lecturers and started out loudly and strongly . . . and then it was pretty much downhill from there. I hung my head.

We briefed our kids on the do's and don'ts of *marae* life and we were all on the page, snuggled up in the *whare* (sleeping house), having got over the *powhiri*. I was glad to be finally peacefully asleep. The thing is that not all young people go to sleep at night. And some, despite warnings, decided to have sneaky feeds and drinks, despite the clear rules of no food and drink in the *whare*. In the morning, I woke to a horrific sight of a large orange stain in the middle of the carpet, right in the area where we were not to have food. I still have a concrete stomach as I remember that moment. I had to face up to my lecturers, and I had to listen to the angry students go on and on about it in the weeks to come. It's not that it didn't matter, it did! To this day there is a nice mat on the floor right there where the "Pākehās came and had a party in our *whare*."

But giving up was not an option. It was hard, but the issues remained and the invitation from God remained too. From there we ventured up north to the heart of Tuhoe land. Our city kids had their mouths open wide as we drove into this other world, uncomfortable, scary. We forgot our *korero* (speech) and sang out of time. We offended the elders and risked antagonizing the activists (Justin just happened to be wearing his Fletcher Challenge marathon t-shirt and they were the ones deforesting the Māori land, uninvited . . . oops!) But something happened to us there that changed our insides, ignited our passion.

We had the privilege of walking with an elder from the *marae* up his mountain. He had never actually walked to the summit before. With two walking sticks and a set of newish hips, we knew this wasn't going to be easy, but his young people walked with him slowly step by step, hour after hour. Those of us who arrived at the top first sat down to watch as the speck of an old man came slowly towards us with his young people surrounding him. This was not ordinary, it was extraordinary. It was beautiful. As he neared the top the young people gathered and did the loudest, proudest *haka* (war dance), pulling him like a *waka* from the water.

He then spoke, telling us of his people's plight, the airstrip that was built on the graves on his old people, the native forest that was destroyed for corporate gains. He spoke of his people struggling in a world dominated by Pākehā values. But he also spoke of his faith in God, his knowledge of God's work amongst us, his appreciation for those who worked with the young people.

From there we had others join us who are Māori, which hasn't been easy for any of us. We think differently, act differently, and struggle to understand each other. But Māori culture has offered us a new way of seeing education, health, spirituality, family, belonging, and God.

Many of us have taken time to learn *te reo Māori* (the Māori language) because we know it is key in our understanding and relating together. Being the only Pākehā in a week-long immersion is uncomfortable, but it helped us realize what it's like for Māori students in the Pākehā system. Each year we go to the *marae*. Each year we try to make progress in our knowledge and understanding. Many of our Māori friends in Urban

Vision have left to work in a Māori community or context, but we remain committed friends—and we remain committed to the journey itself.

We often find ourselves between the two worlds and we are committed to building those bridges. How sad it is that even in the church the cultural divide seems too large to cross. How costly for Pākehā to humble themselves and do what it takes to come as learners, listeners. How costly for our unity and peace, for the justice of the kingdom if we don't.

We have good friends who have relocated to some land near us with a passion to live peacefully with the land and give witness to an alternative way from consumerism. They eat what they grow organically or find thrown in the dumpsters. They refuse to shop. They wear second-hand clothes and use old furniture. They are hospitable to many folk, often those from painful backgrounds. They love friends and celebrations and feasting at times, but they are happy with a quieter, slower way of life. It inspires me. I think of them as I shop now, and it helps me shop less. They help me make better eating choices.

Other friends in Thailand live with the poor in the slums and help the people share life round the community center and local church. They started a jewelry co-op among the women and help them sell their jewelry within the Western markets (selling to the same shops our local friends avoid!), helping to alleviate their poverty and bringing them together as friends. Both are passionate and committed in their sacrificial love, and both responses, though contradictory in some ways, please the heart of God.

Too often the church and even the radical edge of the church have a huge divide between the "right" and "wrong" approach, between this tradition and that, between the place or priority of these gifts and those. At Ngatiawa we are choosing to close some of those historical divides. When a young youth worker was staying recently, he sang that great 70s number, "we are one in the spirit, we are one in the Lord . . . and they'll know we are Christians by our love, by our love," with a raspy voice and some flashy guitar chords, and it really came alive for us again. Maybe it's a song that lives on because it's a challenging truth.

Allowing for differences is not only healthy, it is vital to our being the functional body of Christ. And digging for gold, new truth from all over the place, has made us a lot richer.

Don't Miss the Point

- There is truth across the kingdom in many different shapes.

- Unity is a high value.

- Cultural divides need us to journey the costly road of reconciliation.

- Consent is easier than consensus and often allows us to hold together.

- Issues to break fellowship over are scarce.

- Drawing from the gifts in different parts of the body brings health and maturity.

Look Into It

1 Corinthians 12:12–31
Ask yourself: Which members of the body is God challenging you to appreciate more? What do you offer the body? How do you offer this?

FOURTEEN

The Kingdom Life:
Taking on Kingdom Moments

Recently we had a visit from our friends at L'arche, folks who share their lives and homes with the "core members" who have profound disabilities. Together they have a contagious fun and caring vibe, and we love to have them over for a bit of a tea party.

When they arrived, another family was visiting, whose children were not so confident with Kim, one of the core members. They began laughing at her as she bounced on the trampoline, but the Ngatiawa kids were indignant and soon challenged, "Don't laugh at her!" Instead they formed a circle around her on the trampoline, clapping in time and calling her name. Kim bounced higher and her smile got broader. "Go Kim, go Kim, go Kim . . ." Soon the visiting children were joining in as well. "Jenny," said Brenda, "that is a kingdom moment!" "What's a kingdom moment?" our other friend asked. "How many months have you lived here?" asked Brenda. "I can't believe you don't know what a kingdom moment is!" I realized that it is part of our culture in Urban Vision to notice kingdom moments and share them with each other.

We have learnt to look for the kingdom breaking in, heaven coming here on earth. We try to notice things happening that are part of God's transformation. We notice things growing and changing in our own lives and in the lives of others around us, on the land and in our society. We want to see, hear, and feel the good news. Sometimes it's easier to notice the bad news where evil, violence, or anti-gospel work is spreading. But we are disciplined in our desire to see the good news. We point it out to each other, talk about these "kingdom moments" (another Dave Andrewsism).

Sometimes we take the time to mark these kingdom moments. After finding Jesus in the punk scene, Brenda always felt a little on the out of straight Sunday church, but then she found a place in our community, first working with us in the girls' home, then in the inner city, and later on the land. When she was ready to be baptized, we all helped her prepare, both internally and externally. As a single person, the wedding imagery was important for Brenda so she chose a long, white, not-very-punk dress to wear. Quite possibly she had chunky boots and freaky tights underneath. We gathered at the top of our property, then walked down to the rocky, dry creek bed as Justin explained the symbolism of Brenda's journey, which had been rocky yet faithful, accompanied by the many gathered there that night. Some sang a Negro spiritual (an *O Brother Where Art Thou?*-inspired moment) and small candles illuminated the surrounding bush. On arriving at the river, we baptized her and then gathered around her to pray—a well-marked kingdom moment.

Marking the moments of the kingdom breaking in around us is a primary calling of our community, whether it's a job our unemployed friend has got, a skill someone has learned, a new way of dealing with conflict someone has practiced, a season free of addiction, a new relationship, a reconciled relationship, a harvested crop, a victorious soccer team, or just a magnificent effort put forth. This process is proactive, creative, and intentional. We create the sacred space, call attention to the right place and person, and mark the moments where God has come to dwell among us again. Some of our friends have never had a birthday party or Christmas stocking before. Some have never heard "congratulations" for a job well done. These things that bring joy to God's heart need to be noticed and marked, but it doesn't take lots of money. It can be a special plate to eat from, a bunch of flowers, a certificate, a prayer, a speech, a party, a home-made gift, a cake, a book of photos, a candle, a song, a toast, a banner. These times are inclusive, cheap and unique, creative and often fun.

Early on in our community we also learnt the art of lament. There are times when we light the candles, dim the lights, and weep, wail, cry out to God in our anger, despair, and grief. Getting involved is to share the pain out there, and it's overwhelming for us at times. How full of lament our Scriptures are, an art we have often lost in our Sunday church. But we can create the space that allows it to happen so that we can experience relief and answered prayers.

When Justin's mum was diagnosed with cancer, she agreed to come and stay with us as she prepared to face the end of her life. Her illness caused her to experience psychotic symptoms at times and also kept her from sleeping at appropriate times, so she fitted well into our world in the middle of the city. Our friends from the street community were happy to chat and visit in the middle of the night, and we watched this private person, who had always lived alone and had been reluctant to be involved with any church or faith activity, enjoy community life for the first time. Through this process of becoming vulnerable, she came to recognize herself as God's precious child and to embrace a new faith of hope and reassurance.

At her passing, we painted her coffin with her art students and hosted family and friends to come be with us as we prepared for her burial. Each night there was time to share, cry, laugh, be angry with her, be grateful for her, and remember her. On the last day we awoke at dawn to a beautiful sunrise and closed the lid to Māori *karanga* and prayer. Later in the day we had the funeral and buried her, sharing a cup of tea at her favorite Cosmopolitan club (complete with pokies), then returning to bless the house with God's peace, sharing both pain and beauty with corporate types, artists, public servants, teachers, alcoholics, and prostitutes.

I sense a lot of partying in heaven when sinners repent, when justice comes, when love is extended, and I also sense a lot of grieving when we destroy and tear down the beauty of God's kingdom, or when we miss the kingdom moments. Jesus was a master at marking the moments: the temple scene, the moment when Mary washes his feet. Jesus didn't miss it, "Yeah whatever would someone pass the bread down please?" He marked it. I have come to understand these kingdom occasions as the abundant life that Jesus promised us. There have been so many wonderful times. Our cup really has flown over.

When Aaron arrived to join our community, he wasn't sure what to expect. He was coming in from a different direction from the fast-lane, Auckland city scene of flash big church. Looking for something new he had met Justin. Although very different characters, they had become instantly close friends, but his decision to move down was a shock to us and quite courageous. He laughed it off, saying, "I've told my friends I'm moving to some freakin' weirdo commune, but that my bedroom will be under a waterfall." On his arrival it was too easy not to take him for a ride. We dressed in cloth, painted our faces, and gathered in dimly lit silence. We chanted in other languages (he didn't dare laugh) and rang a bell. We tied a frozen pig to a stake and walked round our prayer labyrinth. We then returned inside, lights on, cup of tea as if nothing had happened. Hilarious! We even made him up a bed outside next to our overflow pipe "waterfall." We love to reminisce over that legend—a little dramatic, but then so was he. In community life we can create the alternative so many people are looking for. The fun and the freaky are part of the joy of it all.

Nowadays, on Thursday nights we gather as a community for tea parties. The table is set with cloth, fancy cups, and saucers (op shop of course), candles. Pots are warmed, visitors invited. We "pour the love" for each other and take turns answering a question: childhood memories, secret dreams, hopes of heaven, UFOs . . .

I love the color that is possible in this life. I have a friend, a solid, church-going Christian, who commented on how hard she finds it to pray these days because she can't really think what to pray for. How can we not be bursting with so much pain and joy and hopes and dreams and questions and searching that we have to discipline ourselves to actually listen during prayer time? So many Christians are living in this "bland land," but my heart screams out, "There is more!"

But we have to host the coming of God's Spirit. We create the alternatives. We notice the kingdom moments and we mark them. What a privilege!

Don't Miss the Point

- We create the alternative which allows God's kingdom to come.

- We make space for joy and celebration.

- We make space for lament and grief.

- We notice and mark moments of transformation.

- Our way as followers is inclusive, simple, and creative.

LOOK INTO IT

Mark 12:41–44
Ask yourself: Where have I noticed a kingdom moment recently? How can I mark a kingdom moment for others to notice?

PART THREE

Launching

Preparing for the Journey: Gathering a Crew, Knowing Your Destination, Charting a Course

After we had been doing youth work for a few years I remember a group of us heading away for the weekend. There were those in our youth work team doing club with us, and we'd also invited others from our neighborhood and church who had been enjoying throwing around the issues of community and involvement over coffee for a while. Someone had booked us a place out on the wild coast on the eastern side of Wellington, and as usual it was too wild to really go outside. But really we could have been anywhere anyway because we were inside plotting together on our new revolution. We threw round ideas until late in the night, ate good food (and it was vegetarian, which was a new idea for us back then), and I remember coming home feeling like something had been started. I remember there being a small group of us, but not just Justin and me anymore. I remember the feeling that as we talked and shared ideas we began to share a real vision for our neighborhood. And we also managed to get some ideas together about how we were actually going to make it happen, or at least some first steps. We were all feeling committed to the youth in our neighborhood, and Justin and I wanted to keep going with our club work. But a few of our friends were feeling particularly passionate about environmental issues and justice and wanted to have a go at working with this focus with a group of kids. Another friend was a fabulous musician, and he talked about forming a group around his interest in the performing arts. A young couple said they would like to make their home available for supportive accommodation. In fact, what I didn't realize is that we had stumbled across getting together what it takes to make something happen.

Nowadays as we meet others and share stories, dream the dream again, they often ask for help about how to get started. What does it take to begin a healthy Christian community that can bring about a kingdom agenda? As we've responded to this question time and time again, we've gathered our answers from what we did well, what we did terribly, and what we have observed both ways in many others.

Basically, we conclude you need three things: a crew (the team), a destination (the dream), and a course to get you there (the scheme).

THE TEAM: GATHERING A CREW

One year the national elections were held right in the middle of our annual *hui* for Urban Vision. We were torn as to whether or not to organize coverage of it for one simple reason: there was so much political difference among us, we weren't sure if it would it be a good time. We did watch it together, and as I looked around the room I remember thinking to myself what a diverse bunch we were. Not only did we have different political agendas, we were different genders, cultures, and tastes in so many things. But we shared our taste for good times in our neighborhood, our preference for each other over other friendships, and our commonality was in Jesus. We didn't need to be the same in every way but we did need each other.

Going it alone is unscriptural and foolish. You're not enough to offer the world, and you won't survive anyhow, so it's important to have a group of people on board. We've also learnt that it's better to gather a small team, with everyone on the same page, than a large one, with everyone only kind of into it. It's important to understand and acknowledge the roles and gifts that each person brings. Not everyone needs to function the same way, but everyone needs to function. In the early days, in particular, it's important to have a group of really committed people if you're going to see something take off. Within that, you need at least a few who can adopt the mantra, "whatever it takes to make this happen, I'll do it."

We now know that pioneering something new is hard, so our advice is usually to apprentice to something else first, somewhere there's support and space for you to join others. Go and be part of another community for awhile or join in with an internship or exposure course. While you're learning with others, you'll discover whether or not you have a pioneer within you or among you. It's okay to serve another dream for a while. Some of our dreams incubated for many years as we were faithful to other seasons first. Some are still hatching!

We did our early years with Youth for Christ, and I am forever grateful for the time we spent alongside others who had been working with kids in the community while we were still riding our tricycles. There were so many things we took on from those years even though our actual involvement these days is vastly different. Just the other day we learnt that the government funding for the Youth Quest employment program we're involved in will be cut in four months time. As I sat with some shattered young people and their mentors, I remembered straight away that "we do what God calls us to do with or without the funding," a solid theme of my early YFC discipleship, there for me still when I need it today.

Leadership is a vital issue we needed to nut through together as a team. We had conservative church goers looking for a pastor to tell them what to do and asking questions of "covering," mixed in with anarchists (christi-anarchists) who only wanted covering to mean that everyone was included in decisions with shared power. Add to this those of us who had been hurt by irresponsible or unsafe leadership and those who lacked the courage to do anything differently from church and you get a right royal (apologies, anarchists) mess. We had to work this through over the years, trying to peel back our own experiences, look for healthy models, and understand what on earth the Scripture actually offers us here and now on this one.

Models of leadership vary, even within the Bible, but you'll need to be in unity about how you're called and convicted to function and support leadership. As cynical kiwis, we are naturally a little adverse towards leadership since we weld it to the abuse of power, so this has been hard for us. But we've worked hard to change the culture within Urban Vision from "protecting ourselves from unsafe leadership" towards "welcoming healthy leadership as a gift offered to us." We have landed with a model of shared power, good communication, and servant leadership.

Related to leadership are the issues of power and decision making. We try to share power, as we know well its potential to corrupt us, but that power is shared by the ones who are paying the price in their commitment. Folks who have just arrived and are likely to be leaving soon don't have much power over the future, since they aren't committed to it, and we don't want to end up having the tail wag the dog. But we are conscious to include both younger and older ones, because our life and health depends on it.

Once we'd gathered a solid team, we could create space for others to gather round the edges. Some people have huge commitments and still want to connect with community and involvement. Some people need to have a look first, dip their toes in before plunging. But we found that if you have too many on the edge and not enough in the center, there will be nothing to inspire and learn from. If there are lots of others sucking time and energy out but not putting time and energy in, the struggling ones in your neighborhood will miss out, same as always.

The key to avoiding most conflict in the team is good communication, with clear expectations and roles, a willingness to negotiate, and an openness to ongoing conversation. As a volunteer, bi-vocational group, time is our most precious resource, so we've worked hard to build an atmosphere of well-earned trust, which allows plenty of freedom and avoids team meetings over the flavor of tea tonight—how exhausting! One general principal we go by is that those who are affected by our decisions have the right to participate in those decisions.

Learning how to prevent and deal with conflict within the team is an absolute must for our community life. But maintaining our own walk with Jesus has been the most vital aspect of health for any team, because: it allows us to access his fruit; it allows us to work on our wholeness/transformation while also supporting this for others; and it allows us to reflect his character of wisdom, grace, and forgiveness vital in resolving conflict.

One day a friend from our community came to us with an issue that had been upsetting him about the way we were functioning. We were able to listen, he was able to tell us gently, with plenty of reassurance. We negotiated a way forward and agreed on what would be better. We apologized, and he thanked us for working it through. He said (and I still can't quite believe this) that "it was a pleasure doing conflict with you." The fact that it stands out as a story may tell you that not all conflict I have experienced in community has been that easy. We are full of the scars of conflict done badly and have caused this scarring on others. But we do believe it's possible, and I hold his quote in my head as I go into conflict now. Conflict is inevitable and can be the most constructive times of growth. Occasionally it can even be a pleasure. When I think of those who have left over conflict I feel so saddened. We try to commit to leaving the community in times of strength and unity rather than when things go bad. The miracle for us is not that we have survived through the conflict with those who have left. The greater miracle is that we are still such close friends with those who have stayed all this time.

The Dream: Knowing Your Destination

Pulling a team together is the start, but without a dream the people will perish, which for us usually means getting distracted and back into the cultural tide. So once we had gathered a team, we needed to establish the dream together so that it would be owned and shared by everyone.

One of our most beautiful dreams is the Te Whare Atawhai girls home. We inherited the dream from Te Ora Hou, who had started the home in our neighborhood to accommodate the girls in their neighborhood who couldn't stay at home safely. We loved our season at the home, and the dream was a clear one for others to grasp and run with. It was clear to young adults who lived with us that our girls needed and deserved what they missed from their families. They needed distraction from the unhealthy habits, and they needed belonging and activity to channel their youthful energy well. Over the years, I watched both the young adults who came to serve, along with the girls themselves, catch the dream and run with it. One young woman who is still a close friend of our family told me that in her darkest hours, it was our including her in the Te Whare Atawhai dream that kept her going forward. She liked to imagine that she could help the other girls who were struggling, that she would one day be a leader in the home.

From our experience, communities who last the distance are those with a strong and clear sense of purpose and calling. The dream we share needs to be big enough to have scope for all sorts of responses, but specific and humble enough to hold us together and ensure that something actually happens. If we aim at everything and everyone, we'll hit nothing and help no one. There are many great kingdom dreams, and we begin the process by listening and holding things lightly.

Some people may not be able to come up with a list of possible dreams, so you'll need to get the dreamers and the visionaries to help you start firing. Find someone who has lived and led the revolution and get them to spend time with you. Or go spend some time where it's already happening, with folks who are going your way, and learn by osmosis. Even if it is not quite the fit for you, being part of a functional community for a while is incredibly valuable. Even after all these years we learn so much when we go and spend time with others who are living out the dream in a different context.

If you have a dream for young adults who are struggling, prisoners who are rehabilitating or mental health consumers, you might begin there and then pray for a location to fit that. Being prayerful helps us avoid choosing the coolest or easiest spot and allows God space to give us some new ideas. In our youth work days, we began by looking round for the best spot to connect with them. Then with each new season, we would walk round, pray, fast, and ask round, observing and sensing God's lead as we went. In narrowing it down, we land with some of us in the neighborhood, prepared to move again if and when we need to.

Once you have a team and a dream, you head towards getting it happening on the ground.

The following is a guide of questions we've found helpful in gathering a household around a dream:

- What is the dream of this household? Why does this household exist?
- Who can live here with us?
- What does it mean to live here?
- What are the expectations daily/weekly/monthly?
- Which expectations are hopes and which are vital?
- Where do we belong?
- Who will support/mentor this household?
- What will their role be?

- How will leadership work here?
- How are decisions made?
- How will the money work?
- What do we believe and commit to around the issue of conflict?
- How will we sustain this over time to be healthy?
- How will we know when it's time to finish/close?
- How will we do this well?
- Are there models of this we can learn from?
- Shall we apprentice ourselves somewhere first?
- What kind of commitment will this take?
- Who will make this commitment?

THE SCHEME: CHARTING A COURSE

A few years ago friends of ours moved into the high-density council flats that are available to low income people. Everyone is there: families, singles, old people, youth, refugees and immigrants, Māori and Pākehā, mental-health consumers and addicts. Their first response was just to be there and get to know the place. Early on they realized that there were lots of young mums and no play group functioning. They were able to gather a few of the mums together and get some funding to get something started. They went for a weekly meeting, but nowadays it's so popular that they meet more often and employ a local mum to run things. It gave them something to do with their neighbors that built up their relationships.

They also noticed that someone was working to get community gardens going, so they made a regular commitment to keeping a plot there going. They didn't need to initiate this, but they chose to support it, and through that built friendships. In time they have become involved in tenancy groups but when it felt unhelpful to the dynamics for them to have too many roles there, they pulled back. All the time they are looking for ways to be helpful to God's kingdom agenda in their neighborhood. Sometimes it involves initiating things, sometimes it involves supporting others' initiative.

Our scheme charts the course we'll take to reach our destination, to reach our dream in our location. But when we make such a plan, we need to hold it lightly before God. There is a balance between making it happen and letting it happen. We will naturally gravitate towards one of these and will need to balance ourselves. I have had to learn to hold my great schemes lightly. Sometimes God doesn't realize what good ideas I've had! I've had to let those ideas go. Others in our community have had to learn how to get on and actually make something happen. Those who have rocked up later often don't realize how much energy it takes to make something happen.

Our scheme usually begins with being available to our neighbors. From there a need arises, and we are in the privileged position to be able to respond. We then work with our neighbors or young people to meet the need in an empowering way. Whether it's a homework club, a gardening project, an employment scheme, or a mother's group, needs and possibilities are endless in a colorful neighborhood.

We are always listening, attending, dreaming, responding, reflecting, and responding again. We have to take others with us on the journey, allowing each other's skills and ideas to develop. We have to allow the gifts to operate. We need the dreamers to dream, the prophets to imagine, the leaders to lead. We need to let those who make it practical tie down the details and help make it a reality. We need the "people people" to hear from others and bring folks on the edges on board. We need to respond to the people we are serving. There are always better and worse ways to respond, so getting your head round some good community development principles is vital. Finally, we need to be faithful to our sense of call and the gifts and passions we carry.

SIXTEEN

The Shape:
Building a Boat

As our community developed around our dream, we needed to decide on the shape of the boat that would hold us and carry our unique dream and calling, encouraging ownership and passion among the whole team. As we searched many community models, we learned how many biblical shapes there are, each with strengths and weaknesses. Slow to connect to a shape, we were known to our YFC friends for a long time as "the latte club," due to our habit of intense communication over coffee. We needed something a bit better than this.

Coming to agreement about a shape is often difficult, and the longer it is left unclarified, the more likely it is to cause tension. Sometimes a movement grows and develops, finds new inspiration, and then needs to adjust its shape again, a process that is both refreshing and painful.

The shape we share in Urban Vision fits into New Monasticism, a movement that has been growing in recent years, particularly in the Western world. And while some are tempted, we don't go for robes. We have found it a helpful, clarifying, and inspiring frame, as it has connected us with lots of like-minded people who are exploring new ways that church can be lived out, bringing the spirit of the old monastics into a modern context. As a model of intentionality, commitment, and focused passion underpinned by a life of prayer and reflection, New Monasticism allows for different expressions of service while holding to a common vision and sense of belonging.

The 12 Marks of New Monasticism are:

1. Relocation to the "abandoned places of Empire" [at the margins of society]

2. Sharing economic resources with fellow community members and the needy among us

3. Hospitality to the stranger

4. Lament for racial divisions within the church and our communities combined with the active pursuit of a just reconciliation

5. Humble submission to Christ's body, the Church

6. Intentional formation in the way of Christ and the rule of the community along the lines of the old novitiate

7. Nurturing common life among members of intentional community

8. Support for celibate singles alongside monogamous married couples and their children

9. Geographical proximity to community members who share a common rule of life

10. Care for the plot of God's earth given to us along with support of our local economies

11. Peacemaking in the midst of violence and conflict resolution within communities along the lines of Matthew 18

12. Commitment to a disciplined contemplative life

Within Urban Vision, we each commit to the community (initially for a year at a time) and to remaining faithful to our unique call. Each of our teams responds differently to their own context, and each individual responds differently within their own team, but the fiber remains the same across us, the same as it's always been. Within that we listen and pray individually about where we are heading and what the next steps on our journey may be. Sometimes there is an area of personal transformation we are working towards, sometime an area in our neighborhood we are growing a passion for, sometimes a focus on a conflict or friendship within our team. Each month, we catch up with our alongsider person for mentoring and support.

During the first few years, people who join us are supported through a formation process, catching up on the readings, the dialogue, and the experiences others have had over the years. After those formative years, people may be led to commit for longer, at which point they become part of the decision making and direction of the movement. For some, Urban Vision is a place to be for a while, to learn and experiment. For others, we have the privilege of growing old together. It is fragile and always changing, but we have all grown and the movement has grown, with around fifty young adults committing each year.

There are plenty of shapes to build your boat and resources around (books, people, exposure courses) that can help you think it out.

SEVENTEEN

The Wider Church:
Paddling in Sync

Communities like Urban Vision often draw those who are over church as we know it. Many of us have a residual groan as we imagine more long hours on the pew listening to a sermon which probably won't change our lives before the lukewarm tea is served. In fact, we would recommend our own little church in the country that has services in under an hour and often finishes with Devonshire tea at the pottery cafe across the road. Funnily, Justin suddenly became very Anglican after this experience.

But having a strong tie to the wider church allows for good support and resourcing in all sorts of ways. First, the community remains aware of what the Spirit is doing in the wider body. Second, being part of the wider church opens a pathway for those who want to join the community as well as those who want to leave it. Third, it bears witness to an alternative model of discipleship and involvement for people within the church, encouraging a healthy dialogue between the edge and the center. Fourth, it allows others to speak into the life of a community more readily. Finally, it extends the gift of the community to the wider body.

At the same time, if people feel pressured to participate fully in the life of the wider congregation, this can draw valuable time and energy away from the dream of the community and the people with whom they are sharing life. People who aren't able to participate fully in church life may end up feeling like second class congregation members. Some churches might not agree with the choices and lifestyle of the community, such as the decision of some families to live in rough neighborhoods and earn little money. If people within the church feel threatened by a community, they may try to draw people away from it or stir up tensions within those who feel called to stay.

Within Urban Vision, we have positioned ourselves on the edge of the institutional church, connecting broadly with the Anglican Church and remaining ecumenical in our flavor. This allows us to be owned by the church on a good day and disowned at times of tension (such as when our social actions become too radical). It ensures that we are aware of what God is doing in other parts of the body, and it keeps us humble to be part of the church, even with all its flaws. Our friends in God Squad quote John Smith, saying, "The church may be a whore but she's my mother!"

Situating ourselves at the back of the church is important (thanks Dave Andrews), because we think this helps the "front focused" church turn round and look out more, encouraging them to consider models where the worship team and the program promoted from the front are not necessarily the priority. Positioning ourselves in this way, we can look for the people within the church who are seeking an alternative model, and we can encourage the rest of the church to move towards community and involvement. This allows us to be part of an ongoing dialogue about the issues we struggle with, so that we can have a prophetic voice while at the same time remaining open to challenge and critique.

As we have connected with our local church, we have also learned from and been inspired by many communities, some historical, some current, some here in New Zealand, and some overseas. You might want to check out:

- Servants to Asia's Urban Poor
- Catholic Worker Movement
- Urban Neighbourhoods of Hope, Melbourne, Bangkok
- Youth for Christ/Incedo, New Zealand
- Te Ora Hou, New Zealand
- Living Well, Wellington
- L'arche, New Zealand
- Waiter's Union, Brisbane

- Community of the Transfiguration, Melbourne
- Inner Change, London, Cambodia, LA
- Mennonite Communities
- God Squad, Wellington
- Stillwaters, Wellington
- A Rocha
- Holy Hill Hermitage, Ireland
- Taize, France
- Iona, Scotland
- Northumbria Community, UK
- Simple Way, Philadelphia
- Psalters, Philadelphia
- Partners, Thailand
- St Stephens Ministry, Hong Kong
- Addington, Christchurch
- Vainga's friends in Dunedin
- Peace Tree, Perth
- Steiger, Mineapolis
- Jacob's Well, Vancouver
- Nieu Communities, Vancouver

Getting into the mix with other groups on a similar *waka*—by staying in other communities, going to missional conferences, and forming friendships with others on the journey—really helps. For us this has not always been easy. I remember hearing of a community set up in the middle of the red light area of another New Zealand city as we were planning to move into our inner-city neighborhood. The guy leading the community was busy and clearly not wanting Christian tourists. He said he was too busy on the phone. We called in anyway. It meant leaving friends in the car double-parked downstairs (turned out to be more than an hour, getting hit on by transvestites), which meant we had to then shout them out for supper afterwards to make up. But we found out what we needed to know. In taking our young people to visit a community in Melbourne, two of them ended up in hospital after eating the new unknown food we had encouraged them to buy at the local market. We didn't know the seeds were poisonous; it looked like the right part to eat. It's risky exploring. It's embarrassing tracking others down. But we have found our connection outside of Urban Vision vital training in how to row this *waka*.

EIGHTEEN

The Provisions:
Sustaining the Journey

From the miracle of beginning a community, we have now been working out to how to sustain it. As time goes on, new issues rise within a community, and we will need to have enough vitality to keep going, even if the journey is hard, even if the weather is foul, even if we fall overboard.

Following are some things we've learned along the way that have helped sustain us for the journey:

- Having a shape that is robust but allows for new creativity.

- Handing ownership and leadership to the next generation.

- Allowing people to grow old well within the movement.

- Allowing children and young people to flourish in the community.

- Allowing others to leave and begin new movements and then work together in unity.

- Coping with all the pain and struggle without losing our souls.

- Processing trauma well.

- Facing our failures, learning from them, discovering new confidence, and carrying on.

- Skillfully handling the complexities of healing and transformation.

- Skillfully managing conflict and non-violence at all levels.

- Developing a model of leadership that is biblical and contextual.

- Knowing the charism of the community and the limits what we offer our neighborhood.

- Understanding the gifts, temperaments, and personalities of our team.

- Having outside mentors to counsel, encourage, and challenge us over the years.

In addition to these guiding principles, we are sustained by regular rhythms of rest and reflection together, along with our commitment to Sabbath keeping. Our old timers all have sabbatical seasons, and our small order takes time each year to hear from God for guidance and direction.

NINETEEN

On the *Waka* in the Wake of Jesus

If you're anything like us, just the thought of those folk who got into small boats and headed for the strange land long ago makes your anxiety levels begin to rise. Where do we get that kind of courage? To leave behind that which is familiar, comfortable, safe, and known for . . . for who knows what? Obviously there was something out there that drew them, or was it that things on their familiar land weren't enough to keep them there? Looking back to our safe land, we realize there is not enough for us to stay. Not enough justice, not enough peace, not enough depth, not enough hope, not enough purpose, not enough adventure. And looking out across the water, we are drawn by him. The kingdom in its fullness is on our horizon, and the kingdom comes with each stroke we row. Our journey like the early travelers to our land, like the travelers throughout the Scriptures, is taking us from the known to the unknown. But we follow in the wake of Jesus, who travels before us. That is our only hope, our only guide.

Like the young man from the Moravian community, who with a few of his friends deliberately sold himself into slavery in order to be good news to the slave community. In anguish, his family begged him, down at the docks as they were leaving, to reconsider. But his answer was I must go, "that the lamb may receive his reward for his suffering." He got on the *waka* with courage and determination. We too are motivated by gratitude to the one who got on the *waka* first and pulled us out of the water.

We are not fit enough to paddle far, we do not have enough resources to last long. But wait, look who's in the boat with us . . . the one who calms the storm, the one who pulls up fish to feed us, his friends—the one who walks on water!